C-129 CAREER EXAMINATION SERIES

This is your
PASSBOOK for...

Caseworker I

Test Preparation Study Guide
Questions & Answers

COPYRIGHT NOTICE

This book is SOLELY intended for, is sold ONLY to, and its use is RESTRICTED to individual, bona fide applicants or candidates who qualify by virtue of having seriously filed applications for appropriate license, certificate, professional and/or promotional advancement, higher school matriculation, scholarship, or other legitimate requirements of education and/or governmental authorities.

This book is NOT intended for use, class instruction, tutoring, training, duplication, copying, reprinting, excerption, or adaptation, etc., by:

1) Other publishers
2) Proprietors and/or Instructors of "Coaching" and/or Preparatory Courses
3) Personnel and/or Training Divisions of commercial, industrial, and governmental organizations
4) Schools, colleges, or universities and/or their departments and staffs, including teachers and other personnel
5) Testing Agencies or Bureaus
6) Study groups which seek by the purchase of a single volume to copy and/or duplicate and/or adapt this material for use by the group as a whole without having purchased individual volumes for each of the members of the group
7) Et al.

Such persons would be in violation of appropriate Federal and State statutes.

PROVISION OF LICENSING AGREEMENTS – Recognized educational, commercial, industrial, and governmental institutions and organizations, and others legitimately engaged in educational pursuits, including training, testing, and measurement activities, may address request for a licensing agreement to the copyright owners, who will determine whether, and under what conditions, including fees and charges, the materials in this book may be used them. In other words, a licensing facility exists for the legitimate use of the material in this book on other than an individual basis. However, it is asseverated and affirmed here that the material in this book CANNOT be used without the receipt of the express permission of such a licensing agreement from the Publishers. Inquiries re licensing should be addressed to the company, attention rights and permissions department.

All rights reserved, including the right of reproduction in whole or in part, in any form or by any means, electronic or mechanical, including photocopying, recording, or by any information storage and retrieval system, without permission in writing from the Publisher.

Copyright © 2024 by
National Learning Corporation

212 Michael Drive, Syosset, NY 11791
(516) 921-8888 • www.passbooks.com
E-mail: info@passbooks.com

PUBLISHED IN THE UNITED STATES OF AMERICA

PASSBOOK® SERIES

THE *PASSBOOK® SERIES* has been created to prepare applicants and candidates for the ultimate academic battlefield – the examination room.

At some time in our lives, each and every one of us may be required to take an examination – for validation, matriculation, admission, qualification, registration, certification, or licensure.

Based on the assumption that every applicant or candidate has met the basic formal educational standards, has taken the required number of courses, and read the necessary texts, the *PASSBOOK® SERIES* furnishes the one special preparation which may assure passing with confidence, instead of failing with insecurity. Examination questions – together with answers – are furnished as the basic vehicle for study so that the mysteries of the examination and its compounding difficulties may be eliminated or diminished by a sure method.

This book is meant to help you pass your examination provided that you qualify and are serious in your objective.

The entire field is reviewed through the huge store of content information which is succinctly presented through a provocative and challenging approach – the question-and-answer method.

A climate of success is established by furnishing the correct answers at the end of each test.

You soon learn to recognize types of questions, forms of questions, and patterns of questioning. You may even begin to anticipate expected outcomes.

You perceive that many questions are repeated or adapted so that you can gain acute insights, which may enable you to score many sure points.

You learn how to confront new questions, or types of questions, and to attack them confidently and work out the correct answers.

You note objectives and emphases, and recognize pitfalls and dangers, so that you may make positive educational adjustments.

Moreover, you are kept fully informed in relation to new concepts, methods, practices, and directions in the field.

You discover that you are actually taking the examination all the time: you are preparing for the examination by "taking" an examination, not by reading extraneous and/or supererogatory textbooks.

In short, this PASSBOOK®, used directedly, should be an important factor in helping you to pass your test.

CASEWORKER I

DUTIES:
Performs professional casework in the field of public social welfare. Work involves the primary responsibility to provide social work services for individuals and/or their families, including children, to assist them with their economic, emotional, social and environmental difficulties.
Performs related duties as required.

SCOPE OF THE EXAMINATION
The written test will be designed to test for knowledge, skills, and/or abilities in such areas as:

1. **Establishing and maintaining effective helping relationships in a social casework setting** - These questions test for an understanding of the factors contributing to the development and maintenance of productive client-worker relationships. You will be provided with descriptions of specific client-worker interactions and asked to select the appropriate responses. The questions cover such topics as confidentiality, time management, professional ethics, and referral techniques.

2. **Interviewing (Caseworker)** - These questions test for an understanding of the principles and techniques of interviewing and their application to specific client-worker situations. You will be provided with a series of concrete interviewing situations for which you will be required to select an appropriate course of action based on an analysis of the situation, the application of the information provided, and the ramifications of various interviewing principles and strategies. You will also be asked questions about the interviewing process and various interviewing techniques.

3. **Preparing written material** - These questions test for the ability to present information clearly and accurately and to organize paragraphs logically and comprehensibly. For some questions, you will be given information in two or three sentences followed by four restatements of the information. You must then choose the best version. For other questions, you will be given paragraphs with their sentences out of order. You must then choose, from four suggestions, the best order for the sentences.

HOW TO TAKE A TEST

I. YOU MUST PASS AN EXAMINATION

A. *WHAT EVERY CANDIDATE SHOULD KNOW*

Examination applicants often ask us for help in preparing for the written test. What can I study in advance? What kinds of questions will be asked? How will the test be given? How will the papers be graded?

As an applicant for a civil service examination, you may be wondering about some of these things. Our purpose here is to suggest effective methods of advance study and to describe civil service examinations.

Your chances for success on this examination can be increased if you know how to prepare. Those "pre-examination jitters" can be reduced if you know what to expect. You can even experience an adventure in good citizenship if you know why civil service exams are given.

B. *WHY ARE CIVIL SERVICE EXAMINATIONS GIVEN?*

Civil service examinations are important to you in two ways. As a citizen, you want public jobs filled by employees who know how to do their work. As a job seeker, you want a fair chance to compete for that job on an equal footing with other candidates. The best-known means of accomplishing this two-fold goal is the competitive examination.

Exams are widely publicized throughout the nation. They may be administered for jobs in federal, state, city, municipal, town or village governments or agencies.

Any citizen may apply, with some limitations, such as the age or residence of applicants. Your experience and education may be reviewed to see whether you meet the requirements for the particular examination. When these requirements exist, they are reasonable and applied consistently to all applicants. Thus, a competitive examination may cause you some uneasiness now, but it is your privilege and safeguard.

C. *HOW ARE CIVIL SERVICE EXAMS DEVELOPED?*

Examinations are carefully written by trained technicians who are specialists in the field known as "psychological measurement," in consultation with recognized authorities in the field of work that the test will cover. These experts recommend the subject matter areas or skills to be tested; only those knowledges or skills important to your success on the job are included. The most reliable books and source materials available are used as references. Together, the experts and technicians judge the difficulty level of the questions.

Test technicians know how to phrase questions so that the problem is clearly stated. Their ethics do not permit "trick" or "catch" questions. Questions may have been tried out on sample groups, or subjected to statistical analysis, to determine their usefulness.

Written tests are often used in combination with performance tests, ratings of training and experience, and oral interviews. All of these measures combine to form the best-known means of finding the right person for the right job.

II. HOW TO PASS THE WRITTEN TEST

A. NATURE OF THE EXAMINATION

To prepare intelligently for civil service examinations, you should know how they differ from school examinations you have taken. In school you were assigned certain definite pages to read or subjects to cover. The examination questions were quite detailed and usually emphasized memory. Civil service exams, on the other hand, try to discover your present ability to perform the duties of a position, plus your potentiality to learn these duties. In other words, a civil service exam attempts to predict how successful you will be. Questions cover such a broad area that they cannot be as minute and detailed as school exam questions.

In the public service similar kinds of work, or positions, are grouped together in one "class." This process is known as *position-classification*. All the positions in a class are paid according to the salary range for that class. One class title covers all of these positions, and they are all tested by the same examination.

B. FOUR BASIC STEPS

1) Study the announcement

How, then, can you know what subjects to study? Our best answer is: "Learn as much as possible about the class of positions for which you've applied." The exam will test the knowledge, skills and abilities needed to do the work.

Your most valuable source of information about the position you want is the official exam announcement. This announcement lists the training and experience qualifications. Check these standards and apply only if you come reasonably close to meeting them.

The brief description of the position in the examination announcement offers some clues to the subjects which will be tested. Think about the job itself. Review the duties in your mind. Can you perform them, or are there some in which you are rusty? Fill in the blank spots in your preparation.

Many jurisdictions preview the written test in the exam announcement by including a section called "Knowledge and Abilities Required," "Scope of the Examination," or some similar heading. Here you will find out specifically what fields will be tested.

2) Review your own background

Once you learn in general what the position is all about, and what you need to know to do the work, ask yourself which subjects you already know fairly well and which need improvement. You may wonder whether to concentrate on improving your strong areas or on building some background in your fields of weakness. When the announcement has specified "some knowledge" or "considerable knowledge," or has used adjectives like "beginning principles of…" or "advanced … methods," you can get a clue as to the number and difficulty of questions to be asked in any given field. More questions, and hence broader coverage, would be included for those subjects which are more important in the work. Now weigh your strengths and weaknesses against the job requirements and prepare accordingly.

3) Determine the level of the position

Another way to tell how intensively you should prepare is to understand the level of the job for which you are applying. Is it the entering level? In other words, is this the position in which beginners in a field of work are hired? Or is it an intermediate or advanced level? Sometimes this is indicated by such words as "Junior" or "Senior" in the class title. Other jurisdictions use Roman numerals to designate the level – Clerk I, Clerk II, for example. The word "Supervisor" sometimes appears in the title. If the level is not indicated by the title, check the description of duties. Will you be working under very close supervision, or will you have responsibility for independent decisions in this work?

4) Choose appropriate study materials

Now that you know the subjects to be examined and the relative amount of each subject to be covered, you can choose suitable study materials. For beginning level jobs, or even advanced ones, if you have a pronounced weakness in some aspect of your training, read a modern, standard textbook in that field. Be sure it is up to date and has general coverage. Such books are normally available at your library, and the librarian will be glad to help you locate one. For entry-level positions, questions of appropriate difficulty are chosen – neither highly advanced questions, nor those too simple. Such questions require careful thought but not advanced training.

If the position for which you are applying is technical or advanced, you will read more advanced, specialized material. If you are already familiar with the basic principles of your field, elementary textbooks would waste your time. Concentrate on advanced textbooks and technical periodicals. Think through the concepts and review difficult problems in your field.

These are all general sources. You can get more ideas on your own initiative, following these leads. For example, training manuals and publications of the government agency which employs workers in your field can be useful, particularly for technical and professional positions. A letter or visit to the government department involved may result in more specific study suggestions, and certainly will provide you with a more definite idea of the exact nature of the position you are seeking.

III. KINDS OF TESTS

Tests are used for purposes other than measuring knowledge and ability to perform specified duties. For some positions, it is equally important to test ability to make adjustments to new situations or to profit from training. In others, basic mental abilities not dependent on information are essential. Questions which test these things may not appear as pertinent to the duties of the position as those which test for knowledge and information. Yet they are often highly important parts of a fair examination. For very general questions, it is almost impossible to help you direct your study efforts. What we can do is to point out some of the more common of these general abilities needed in public service positions and describe some typical questions.

1) General information

Broad, general information has been found useful for predicting job success in some kinds of work. This is tested in a variety of ways, from vocabulary lists to questions about current events. Basic background in some field of work, such as sociology or economics, may be sampled in a group of questions. Often these are principles which have become familiar to most persons through exposure rather than through formal training. It is difficult to advise you how to study for these questions; being alert to the world around you is our best suggestion.

2) Verbal ability

An example of an ability needed in many positions is verbal or language ability. Verbal ability is, in brief, the ability to use and understand words. Vocabulary and grammar tests are typical measures of this ability. Reading comprehension or paragraph interpretation questions are common in many kinds of civil service tests. You are given a paragraph of written material and asked to find its central meaning.

3) Numerical ability

Number skills can be tested by the familiar arithmetic problem, by checking paired lists of numbers to see which are alike and which are different, or by interpreting charts and graphs. In the latter test, a graph may be printed in the test booklet which you are asked to use as the basis for answering questions.

4) Observation

A popular test for law-enforcement positions is the observation test. A picture is shown to you for several minutes, then taken away. Questions about the picture test your ability to observe both details and larger elements.

5) Following directions

In many positions in the public service, the employee must be able to carry out written instructions dependably and accurately. You may be given a chart with several columns, each column listing a variety of information. The questions require you to carry out directions involving the information given in the chart.

6) Skills and aptitudes

Performance tests effectively measure some manual skills and aptitudes. When the skill is one in which you are trained, such as typing or shorthand, you can practice. These tests are often very much like those given in business school or high school courses. For many of the other skills and aptitudes, however, no short-time preparation can be made. Skills and abilities natural to you or that you have developed throughout your lifetime are being tested.

Many of the general questions just described provide all the data needed to answer the questions and ask you to use your reasoning ability to find the answers. Your best preparation for these tests, as well as for tests of facts and ideas, is to be at your physical and mental best. You, no doubt, have your own methods of getting into an exam-taking mood and keeping "in shape." The next section lists some ideas on this subject.

IV. KINDS OF QUESTIONS

Only rarely is the "essay" question, which you answer in narrative form, used in civil service tests. Civil service tests are usually of the short-answer type. Full instructions for answering these questions will be given to you at the examination. But in case this is your first experience with short-answer questions and separate answer sheets, here is what you need to know:

1) Multiple-choice Questions

Most popular of the short-answer questions is the "multiple choice" or "best answer" question. It can be used, for example, to test for factual knowledge, ability to solve problems or judgment in meeting situations found at work.

A multiple-choice question is normally one of three types—
- It can begin with an incomplete statement followed by several possible endings. You are to find the one ending which *best* completes the statement, although some of the others may not be entirely wrong.
- It can also be a complete statement in the form of a question which is answered by choosing one of the statements listed.

- It can be in the form of a problem – again you select the best answer.

Here is an example of a multiple-choice question with a discussion which should give you some clues as to the method for choosing the right answer:

When an employee has a complaint about his assignment, the action which will *best* help him overcome his difficulty is to
    A. discuss his difficulty with his coworkers
    B. take the problem to the head of the organization
    C. take the problem to the person who gave him the assignment
    D. say nothing to anyone about his complaint

In answering this question, you should study each of the choices to find which is best. Consider choice "A" – Certainly an employee may discuss his complaint with fellow employees, but no change or improvement can result, and the complaint remains unresolved. Choice "B" is a poor choice since the head of the organization probably does not know what assignment you have been given, and taking your problem to him is known as "going over the head" of the supervisor. The supervisor, or person who made the assignment, is the person who can clarify it or correct any injustice. Choice "C" is, therefore, correct. To say nothing, as in choice "D," is unwise. Supervisors have and interest in knowing the problems employees are facing, and the employee is seeking a solution to his problem.

2) True/False Questions

The "true/false" or "right/wrong" form of question is sometimes used. Here a complete statement is given. Your job is to decide whether the statement is right or wrong.

SAMPLE: A roaming cell-phone call to a nearby city costs less than a non-roaming call to a distant city.

This statement is wrong, or false, since roaming calls are more expensive.

This is not a complete list of all possible question forms, although most of the others are variations of these common types. You will always get complete directions for answering questions. Be sure you understand *how* to mark your answers – ask questions until you do.

V. RECORDING YOUR ANSWERS

Computer terminals are used more and more today for many different kinds of exams.
For an examination with very few applicants, you may be told to record your answers in the test booklet itself. Separate answer sheets are much more common. If this separate answer sheet is to be scored by machine – and this is often the case – it is highly important that you mark your answers correctly in order to get credit.

An electronic scoring machine is often used in civil service offices because of the speed with which papers can be scored. Machine-scored answer sheets must be marked with a pencil, which will be given to you. This pencil has a high graphite content which responds to the electronic scoring machine. As a matter of fact, stray dots may register as answers, so do not let your pencil rest on the answer sheet while you are pondering the correct answer. Also, if your pencil lead breaks or is otherwise defective, ask for another.

Since the answer sheet will be dropped in a slot in the scoring machine, be careful not to bend the corners or get the paper crumpled.

The answer sheet normally has five vertical columns of numbers, with 30 numbers to a column. These numbers correspond to the question numbers in your test booklet. After each number, going across the page are four or five pairs of dotted lines. These short dotted lines have small letters or numbers above them. The first two pairs may also have a "T" or "F" above the letters. This indicates that the first two pairs only are to be used if the questions are of the true-false type. If the questions are multiple choice, disregard the "T" and "F" and pay attention only to the small letters or numbers.

Answer your questions in the manner of the sample that follows:

32. The largest city in the United States is
    A. Washington, D.C.
    B. New York City
    C. Chicago
    D. Detroit
    E. San Francisco

1) Choose the answer you think is best. (New York City is the largest, so "B" is correct.)
2) Find the row of dotted lines numbered the same as the question you are answering. (Find row number 32)
3) Find the pair of dotted lines corresponding to the answer. (Find the pair of lines under the mark "B.")
4) Make a solid black mark between the dotted lines.

VI. BEFORE THE TEST

Common sense will help you find procedures to follow to get ready for an examination. Too many of us, however, overlook these sensible measures. Indeed, nervousness and fatigue have been found to be the most serious reasons why applicants fail to do their best on civil service tests. Here is a list of reminders:

- Begin your preparation early – Don't wait until the last minute to go scurrying around for books and materials or to find out what the position is all about.
- Prepare continuously – An hour a night for a week is better than an all-night cram session. This has been definitely established. What is more, a night a week for a month will return better dividends than crowding your study into a shorter period of time.
- Locate the place of the exam – You have been sent a notice telling you when and where to report for the examination. If the location is in a different town or otherwise unfamiliar to you, it would be well to inquire the best route and learn something about the building.
- Relax the night before the test – Allow your mind to rest. Do not study at all that night. Plan some mild recreation or diversion; then go to bed early and get a good night's sleep.
- Get up early enough to make a leisurely trip to the place for the test – This way unforeseen events, traffic snarls, unfamiliar buildings, etc. will not upset you.
- Dress comfortably – A written test is not a fashion show. You will be known by number and not by name, so wear something comfortable.

- Leave excess paraphernalia at home – Shopping bags and odd bundles will get in your way. You need bring only the items mentioned in the official notice you received; usually everything you need is provided. Do not bring reference books to the exam. They will only confuse those last minutes and be taken away from you when in the test room.
- Arrive somewhat ahead of time – If because of transportation schedules you must get there very early, bring a newspaper or magazine to take your mind off yourself while waiting.
- Locate the examination room – When you have found the proper room, you will be directed to the seat or part of the room where you will sit. Sometimes you are given a sheet of instructions to read while you are waiting. Do not fill out any forms until you are told to do so; just read them and be prepared.
- Relax and prepare to listen to the instructions
- If you have any physical problem that may keep you from doing your best, be sure to tell the test administrator. If you are sick or in poor health, you really cannot do your best on the exam. You can come back and take the test some other time.

VII. AT THE TEST

The day of the test is here and you have the test booklet in your hand. The temptation to get going is very strong. Caution! There is more to success than knowing the right answers. You must know how to identify your papers and understand variations in the type of short-answer question used in this particular examination. Follow these suggestions for maximum results from your efforts:

1) Cooperate with the monitor

The test administrator has a duty to create a situation in which you can be as much at ease as possible. He will give instructions, tell you when to begin, check to see that you are marking your answer sheet correctly, and so on. He is not there to guard you, although he will see that your competitors do not take unfair advantage. He wants to help you do your best.

2) Listen to all instructions

Don't jump the gun! Wait until you understand all directions. In most civil service tests you get more time than you need to answer the questions. So don't be in a hurry. Read each word of instructions until you clearly understand the meaning. Study the examples, listen to all announcements and follow directions. Ask questions if you do not understand what to do.

3) Identify your papers

Civil service exams are usually identified by number only. You will be assigned a number; you must not put your name on your test papers. Be sure to copy your number correctly. Since more than one exam may be given, copy your exact examination title.

4) Plan your time

Unless you are told that a test is a "speed" or "rate of work" test, speed itself is usually not important. Time enough to answer all the questions will be provided, but this does not mean that you have all day. An overall time limit has been set. Divide the total time (in minutes) by the number of questions to determine the approximate time you have for each question.

5) Do not linger over difficult questions

If you come across a difficult question, mark it with a paper clip (useful to have along) and come back to it when you have been through the booklet. One caution if you do this – be sure to skip a number on your answer sheet as well. Check often to be sure that you have not lost your place and that you are marking in the row numbered the same as the question you are answering.

6) Read the questions

Be sure you know what the question asks! Many capable people are unsuccessful because they failed to *read* the questions correctly.

7) Answer all questions

Unless you have been instructed that a penalty will be deducted for incorrect answers, it is better to guess than to omit a question.

8) Speed tests

It is often better NOT to guess on speed tests. It has been found that on timed tests people are tempted to spend the last few seconds before time is called in marking answers at random – without even reading them – in the hope of picking up a few extra points. To discourage this practice, the instructions may warn you that your score will be "corrected" for guessing. That is, a penalty will be applied. The incorrect answers will be deducted from the correct ones, or some other penalty formula will be used.

9) Review your answers

If you finish before time is called, go back to the questions you guessed or omitted to give them further thought. Review other answers if you have time.

10) Return your test materials

If you are ready to leave before others have finished or time is called, take ALL your materials to the monitor and leave quietly. Never take any test material with you. The monitor can discover whose papers are not complete, and taking a test booklet may be grounds for disqualification.

VIII. EXAMINATION TECHNIQUES

1) Read the general instructions carefully. These are usually printed on the first page of the exam booklet. As a rule, these instructions refer to the timing of the examination; the fact that you should not start work until the signal and must stop work at a signal, etc. If there are any *special* instructions, such as a choice of questions to be answered, make sure that you note this instruction carefully.

2) When you are ready to start work on the examination, that is as soon as the signal has been given, read the instructions to each question booklet, underline any key words or phrases, such as *least, best, outline, describe* and the like. In this way you will tend to answer as requested rather than discover on reviewing your paper that you *listed without describing*, that you selected the *worst* choice rather than the *best* choice, etc.

3) If the examination is of the objective or multiple-choice type – that is, each question will also give a series of possible answers: A, B, C or D, and you are called upon to select the best answer and write the letter next to that answer on your answer paper – it is advisable to start answering each question in turn. There may be anywhere from 50 to 100 such questions in the three or four hours allotted and you can see how much time would be taken if you read through all the questions before beginning to answer any. Furthermore, if you come across a question or group of questions which you know would be difficult to answer, it would undoubtedly affect your handling of all the other questions.

4) If the examination is of the essay type and contains but a few questions, it is a moot point as to whether you should read all the questions before starting to answer any one. Of course, if you are given a choice – say five out of seven and the like – then it is essential to read all the questions so you can eliminate the two that are most difficult. If, however, you are asked to answer all the questions, there may be danger in trying to answer the easiest one first because you may find that you will spend too much time on it. The best technique is to answer the first question, then proceed to the second, etc.

5) Time your answers. Before the exam begins, write down the time it started, then add the time allowed for the examination and write down the time it must be completed, then divide the time available somewhat as follows:
    - If 3-1/2 hours are allowed, that would be 210 minutes. If you have 80 objective-type questions, that would be an average of 2-1/2 minutes per question. Allow yourself no more than 2 minutes per question, or a total of 160 minutes, which will permit about 50 minutes to review.
    - If for the time allotment of 210 minutes there are 7 essay questions to answer, that would average about 30 minutes a question. Give yourself only 25 minutes per question so that you have about 35 minutes to review.

6) The most important instruction is to *read each question* and make sure you know what is wanted. The second most important instruction is to *time yourself properly* so that you answer every question. The third most important instruction is to *answer every question*. Guess if you have to but include something for each question. Remember that you will receive no credit for a blank and will probably receive some credit if you write something in answer to an essay question. If you guess a letter – say "B" for a multiple-choice question – you may have guessed right. If you leave a blank as an answer to a multiple-choice question, the examiners may respect your feelings but it will not add a point to your score. Some exams may penalize you for wrong answers, so in such cases *only*, you may not want to guess unless you have some basis for your answer.

7) Suggestions
    a. Objective-type questions
        1. Examine the question booklet for proper sequence of pages and questions
        2. Read all instructions carefully
        3. Skip any question which seems too difficult; return to it after all other questions have been answered
        4. Apportion your time properly; do not spend too much time on any single question or group of questions

5. Note and underline key words – *all, most, fewest, least, best, worst, same, opposite*, etc.
6. Pay particular attention to negatives
7. Note unusual option, e.g., unduly long, short, complex, different or similar in content to the body of the question
8. Observe the use of "hedging" words – *probably, may, most likely*, etc.
9. Make sure that your answer is put next to the same number as the question
10. Do not second-guess unless you have good reason to believe the second answer is definitely more correct
11. Cross out original answer if you decide another answer is more accurate; do not erase until you are ready to hand your paper in
12. Answer all questions; guess unless instructed otherwise
13. Leave time for review

   b. Essay questions
   1. Read each question carefully
   2. Determine exactly what is wanted. Underline key words or phrases.
   3. Decide on outline or paragraph answer
   4. Include many different points and elements unless asked to develop any one or two points or elements
   5. Show impartiality by giving pros and cons unless directed to select one side only
   6. Make and write down any assumptions you find necessary to answer the questions
   7. Watch your English, grammar, punctuation and choice of words
   8. Time your answers; don't crowd material

8) Answering the essay question

Most essay questions can be answered by framing the specific response around several key words or ideas. Here are a few such key words or ideas:

M's: manpower, materials, methods, money, management
P's: purpose, program, policy, plan, procedure, practice, problems, pitfalls, personnel, public relations

   a. Six basic steps in handling problems:
   1. Preliminary plan and background development
   2. Collect information, data and facts
   3. Analyze and interpret information, data and facts
   4. Analyze and develop solutions as well as make recommendations
   5. Prepare report and sell recommendations
   6. Install recommendations and follow up effectiveness

   b. Pitfalls to avoid
   1. *Taking things for granted* – A statement of the situation does not necessarily imply that each of the elements is necessarily true; for example, a complaint may be invalid and biased so that all that can be taken for granted is that a complaint has been registered

2. *Considering only one side of a situation* – Wherever possible, indicate several alternatives and then point out the reasons you selected the best one
3. *Failing to indicate follow up* – Whenever your answer indicates action on your part, make certain that you will take proper follow-up action to see how successful your recommendations, procedures or actions turn out to be
4. *Taking too long in answering any single question* – Remember to time your answers properly

IX. AFTER THE TEST

Scoring procedures differ in detail among civil service jurisdictions although the general principles are the same. Whether the papers are hand-scored or graded by machine we have described, they are nearly always graded by number. That is, the person who marks the paper knows only the number – never the name – of the applicant. Not until all the papers have been graded will they be matched with names. If other tests, such as training and experience or oral interview ratings have been given, scores will be combined. Different parts of the examination usually have different weights. For example, the written test might count 60 percent of the final grade, and a rating of training and experience 40 percent. In many jurisdictions, veterans will have a certain number of points added to their grades.

After the final grade has been determined, the names are placed in grade order and an eligible list is established. There are various methods for resolving ties between those who get the same final grade – probably the most common is to place first the name of the person whose application was received first. Job offers are made from the eligible list in the order the names appear on it. You will be notified of your grade and your rank as soon as all these computations have been made. This will be done as rapidly as possible.

People who are found to meet the requirements in the announcement are called "eligibles." Their names are put on a list of eligible candidates. An eligible's chances of getting a job depend on how high he stands on this list and how fast agencies are filling jobs from the list.

When a job is to be filled from a list of eligibles, the agency asks for the names of people on the list of eligibles for that job. When the civil service commission receives this request, it sends to the agency the names of the three people highest on this list. Or, if the job to be filled has specialized requirements, the office sends the agency the names of the top three persons who meet these requirements from the general list.

The appointing officer makes a choice from among the three people whose names were sent to him. If the selected person accepts the appointment, the names of the others are put back on the list to be considered for future openings.

That is the rule in hiring from all kinds of eligible lists, whether they are for typist, carpenter, chemist, or something else. For every vacancy, the appointing officer has his choice of any one of the top three eligibles on the list. This explains why the person whose name is on top of the list sometimes does not get an appointment when some of the persons lower on the list do. If the appointing officer chooses the second or third eligible, the No. 1 eligible does not get a job at once, but stays on the list until he is appointed or the list is terminated.

X. HOW TO PASS THE INTERVIEW TEST

The examination for which you applied requires an oral interview test. You have already taken the written test and you are now being called for the interview test – the final part of the formal examination.

You may think that it is not possible to prepare for an interview test and that there are no procedures to follow during an interview. Our purpose is to point out some things you can do in advance that will help you and some good rules to follow and pitfalls to avoid while you are being interviewed.

What is an interview supposed to test?

The written examination is designed to test the technical knowledge and competence of the candidate; the oral is designed to evaluate intangible qualities, not readily measured otherwise, and to establish a list showing the relative fitness of each candidate – as measured against his competitors – for the position sought. Scoring is not on the basis of "right" and "wrong," but on a sliding scale of values ranging from "not passable" to "outstanding." As a matter of fact, it is possible to achieve a relatively low score without a single "incorrect" answer because of evident weakness in the qualities being measured.

Occasionally, an examination may consist entirely of an oral test – either an individual or a group oral. In such cases, information is sought concerning the technical knowledges and abilities of the candidate, since there has been no written examination for this purpose. More commonly, however, an oral test is used to supplement a written examination.

Who conducts interviews?

The composition of oral boards varies among different jurisdictions. In nearly all, a representative of the personnel department serves as chairman. One of the members of the board may be a representative of the department in which the candidate would work. In some cases, "outside experts" are used, and, frequently, a businessman or some other representative of the general public is asked to serve. Labor and management or other special groups may be represented. The aim is to secure the services of experts in the appropriate field.

However the board is composed, it is a good idea (and not at all improper or unethical) to ascertain in advance of the interview who the members are and what groups they represent. When you are introduced to them, you will have some idea of their backgrounds and interests, and at least you will not stutter and stammer over their names.

What should be done before the interview?

While knowledge about the board members is useful and takes some of the surprise element out of the interview, there is other preparation which is more substantive. It *is* possible to prepare for an oral interview – in several ways:

1) Keep a copy of your application and review it carefully before the interview

This may be the only document before the oral board, and the starting point of the interview. Know what education and experience you have listed there, and the sequence and dates of all of it. Sometimes the board will ask you to review the highlights of your experience for them; you should not have to hem and haw doing it.

2) Study the class specification and the examination announcement

Usually, the oral board has one or both of these to guide them. The qualities, characteristics or knowledges required by the position sought are stated in these documents. They offer valuable clues as to the nature of the oral interview. For example, if the job involves supervisory responsibilities, the announcement will usually indicate that knowledge of modern supervisory methods and the qualifications of the candidate as a supervisor will be tested. If so, you can expect such questions, frequently in the form of a hypothetical situation which you are expected to solve. NEVER go into an oral without knowledge of the duties and responsibilities of the job you seek.

3) Think through each qualification required

Try to visualize the kind of questions you would ask if you were a board member. How well could you answer them? Try especially to appraise your own knowledge and background in each area, *measured against the job sought*, and identify any areas in which you are weak. Be critical and realistic – do not flatter yourself.

4) Do some general reading in areas in which you feel you may be weak

For example, if the job involves supervision and your past experience has NOT, some general reading in supervisory methods and practices, particularly in the field of human relations, might be useful. Do NOT study agency procedures or detailed manuals. The oral board will be testing your understanding and capacity, not your memory.

5) Get a good night's sleep and watch your general health and mental attitude

You will want a clear head at the interview. Take care of a cold or any other minor ailment, and of course, no hangovers.

What should be done on the day of the interview?

Now comes the day of the interview itself. Give yourself plenty of time to get there. Plan to arrive somewhat ahead of the scheduled time, particularly if your appointment is in the fore part of the day. If a previous candidate fails to appear, the board might be ready for you a bit early. By early afternoon an oral board is almost invariably behind schedule if there are many candidates, and you may have to wait. Take along a book or magazine to read, or your application to review, but leave any extraneous material in the waiting room when you go in for your interview. In any event, relax and compose yourself.

The matter of dress is important. The board is forming impressions about you – from your experience, your manners, your attitude, and your appearance. Give your personal appearance careful attention. Dress your best, but not your flashiest. Choose conservative, appropriate clothing, and be sure it is immaculate. This is a business interview, and your appearance should indicate that you regard it as such. Besides, being well groomed and properly dressed will help boost your confidence.

Sooner or later, someone will call your name and escort you into the interview room. *This is it.* From here on you are on your own. It is too late for any more preparation. But remember, you asked for this opportunity to prove your fitness, and you are here because your request was granted.

What happens when you go in?

The usual sequence of events will be as follows: The clerk (who is often the board stenographer) will introduce you to the chairman of the oral board, who will introduce you to the other members of the board. Acknowledge the introductions before you sit down. Do not be surprised if you find a microphone facing you or a stenotypist sitting by. Oral interviews are usually recorded in the event of an appeal or other review.

Usually the chairman of the board will open the interview by reviewing the highlights of your education and work experience from your application – primarily for the benefit of the other members of the board, as well as to get the material into the record. Do not interrupt or comment unless there is an error or significant misinterpretation; if that is the case, do not hesitate. But do not quibble about insignificant matters. Also, he will usually ask you some question about your education, experience or your present job – partly to get you to start talking and to establish the interviewing "rapport." He may start the actual questioning, or turn it over to one of the other members. Frequently, each member undertakes the questioning on a particular area, one in which he is perhaps most competent, so you can expect each member to participate in the examination. Because time is limited, you may also expect some rather abrupt switches in the direction the questioning takes, so do not be upset by it. Normally, a board member will not pursue a single line of questioning unless he discovers a particular strength or weakness.

After each member has participated, the chairman will usually ask whether any member has any further questions, then will ask you if you have anything you wish to add. Unless you are expecting this question, it may floor you. Worse, it may start you off on an extended, extemporaneous speech. The board is not usually seeking more information. The question is principally to offer you a last opportunity to present further qualifications or to indicate that you have nothing to add. So, if you feel that a significant qualification or characteristic has been overlooked, it is proper to point it out in a sentence or so. Do not compliment the board on the thoroughness of their examination – they have been sketchy, and you know it. If you wish, merely say, "No thank you, I have nothing further to add." This is a point where you can "talk yourself out" of a good impression or fail to present an important bit of information. Remember, *you close the interview yourself*.

The chairman will then say, "That is all, Mr. _____, thank you." Do not be startled; the interview is over, and quicker than you think. Thank him, gather your belongings and take your leave. Save your sigh of relief for the other side of the door.

How to put your best foot forward

Throughout this entire process, you may feel that the board individually and collectively is trying to pierce your defenses, seek out your hidden weaknesses and embarrass and confuse you. Actually, this is not true. They are obliged to make an appraisal of your qualifications for the job you are seeking, and they want to see you in your best light. Remember, they must interview all candidates and a non-cooperative candidate may become a failure in spite of their best efforts to bring out his qualifications. Here are 15 suggestions that will help you:

1) Be natural – Keep your attitude confident, not cocky

If you are not confident that you can do the job, do not expect the board to be. Do not apologize for your weaknesses, try to bring out your strong points. The board is interested in a positive, not negative, presentation. Cockiness will antagonize any board member and make him wonder if you are covering up a weakness by a false show of strength.

2) Get comfortable, but don't lounge or sprawl

Sit erectly but not stiffly. A careless posture may lead the board to conclude that you are careless in other things, or at least that you are not impressed by the importance of the occasion. Either conclusion is natural, even if incorrect. Do not fuss with your clothing, a pencil or an ashtray. Your hands may occasionally be useful to emphasize a point; do not let them become a point of distraction.

3) Do not wisecrack or make small talk

This is a serious situation, and your attitude should show that you consider it as such. Further, the time of the board is limited – they do not want to waste it, and neither should you.

4) Do not exaggerate your experience or abilities

In the first place, from information in the application or other interviews and sources, the board may know more about you than you think. Secondly, you probably will not get away with it. An experienced board is rather adept at spotting such a situation, so do not take the chance.

5) If you know a board member, do not make a point of it, yet do not hide it

Certainly you are not fooling him, and probably not the other members of the board. Do not try to take advantage of your acquaintanceship – it will probably do you little good.

6) Do not dominate the interview

Let the board do that. They will give you the clues – do not assume that you have to do all the talking. Realize that the board has a number of questions to ask you, and do not try to take up all the interview time by showing off your extensive knowledge of the answer to the first one.

7) Be attentive

You only have 20 minutes or so, and you should keep your attention at its sharpest throughout. When a member is addressing a problem or question to you, give him your undivided attention. Address your reply principally to him, but do not exclude the other board members.

8) Do not interrupt

A board member may be stating a problem for you to analyze. He will ask you a question when the time comes. Let him state the problem, and wait for the question.

9) Make sure you understand the question

Do not try to answer until you are sure what the question is. If it is not clear, restate it in your own words or ask the board member to clarify it for you. However, do not haggle about minor elements.

10) Reply promptly but not hastily

A common entry on oral board rating sheets is "candidate responded readily," or "candidate hesitated in replies." Respond as promptly and quickly as you can, but do not jump to a hasty, ill-considered answer.

11) Do not be peremptory in your answers

A brief answer is proper – but do not fire your answer back. That is a losing game from your point of view. The board member can probably ask questions much faster than you can answer them.

12) Do not try to create the answer you think the board member wants

He is interested in what kind of mind you have and how it works – not in playing games. Furthermore, he can usually spot this practice and will actually grade you down on it.

13) Do not switch sides in your reply merely to agree with a board member

Frequently, a member will take a contrary position merely to draw you out and to see if you are willing and able to defend your point of view. Do not start a debate, yet do not surrender a good position. If a position is worth taking, it is worth defending.

14) Do not be afraid to admit an error in judgment if you are shown to be wrong
 The board knows that you are forced to reply without any opportunity for careful consideration. Your answer may be demonstrably wrong. If so, admit it and get on with the interview.

15) Do not dwell at length on your present job
 The opening question may relate to your present assignment. Answer the question but do not go into an extended discussion. You are being examined for a *new* job, not your present one. As a matter of fact, try to phrase ALL your answers in terms of the job for which you are being examined.

Basis of Rating
 Probably you will forget most of these "do's" and "don'ts" when you walk into the oral interview room. Even remembering them all will not ensure you a passing grade. Perhaps you did not have the qualifications in the first place. But remembering them will help you to put your best foot forward, without treading on the toes of the board members.
 Rumor and popular opinion to the contrary notwithstanding, an oral board wants you to make the best appearance possible. They know you are under pressure – but they also want to see how you respond to it as a guide to what your reaction would be under the pressures of the job you seek. They will be influenced by the degree of poise you display, the personal traits you show and the manner in which you respond.

ABOUT THIS BOOK

 This book contains tests divided into Examination Sections. Go through each test, answering every question in the margin. We have also attached a sample answer sheet at the back of the book that can be removed and used. At the end of each test look at the answer key and check your answers. On the ones you got wrong, look at the right answer choice and learn. Do not fill in the answers first. Do not memorize the questions and answers, but understand the answer and principles involved. On your test, the questions will likely be different from the samples. Questions are changed and new ones added. If you understand these past questions you should have success with any changes that arise. Tests may consist of several types of questions. We have additional books on each subject should more study be advisable or necessary for you. Finally, the more you study, the better prepared you will be. This book is intended to be the last thing you study before you walk into the examination room. Prior study of relevant texts is also recommended. NLC publishes some of these in our Fundamental Series. Knowledge and good sense are important factors in passing your exam. Good luck also helps. So now study this Passbook, absorb the material contained within and take that knowledge into the examination. Then do your best to pass that exam.

EXAMINATION SECTION

EXAMINATION SECTION
TEST 1

DIRECTIONS: Each question or incomplete statement is followed by several suggested answers or completions. Select the one that BEST answers the question or completes the statement. *PRINT THE LETTER OF THE CORRECT ANSWER IN THE SPACE AT THE RIGHT.*

1. A client tells you that he is extremely upset by the treatment that he received from Center personnel at the information desk.
   Which of the following is the BEST way to handle this complaint during the interview?
   A. Explain to the client that he probably misinterpreted what occurred at the information desk
   B. Let the client express his feelings and then proceed with the interview
   C. Tell the client that you are not concerned with the personnel at the information desk
   D. Escort the client to the information desk to find out what really happened

1.____

2. As a worker in the foster home division, you are reviewing a case record to determine whether a 13-year-old boy, in foster care because of neglect and mistreatment by his natural parents, should be returned home. The natural parents, who want to take the child back, have been in family counseling, with encouraging result, and have improved their living conditions.
   Of the following, it would be appropriate to recommend that the child
   A. remain with the foster parents, since this is a documented case of child abuse
   B. remain with the foster parents until they are ready to send him home
   C. be returned to his natural parents, since they have made positive efforts to change their behavior toward the child
   D. be returned to his natural parents, because continued separation will cause irreparable damage to the child

2.____

3. You are finishing an interview with a client in which you have explained to her the procedure she must go through to apply for income maintenance.
   Of the following, the BEST way for you to make sure that she has fully understood the procedure is too ask her
   A. whether she feels she has understood your explanation of the procedure
   B. whether she has any questions to ask you about the procedure
   C. to describe the procedure to you in her own words
   D. a few questions to test her understanding of the procedure

3.____

4. Mrs. Carey, a widow with five children, has come to the field office to seek foster care for her 13-year-old daughter, who has often been truant from school and has recently been caught shoplifting. Mrs. Carey says that she cannot maintain a proper home environment for the other four children and deal with her daughter at the same time.

4.____

1

Of the following, you should FIRST
- A. process Mrs. Carey's request for placement of her daughter in a foster care agency
- B. interview both Mrs. Carey and her daughter to get a more complete picture of the situation
- C. suggest to Mrs. Care that she might be able to manage if she obtained homemaker services
- D. warn the daughter that she will be sent away from home if she does not change her behavior

5. During a group orientation meeting with couples who wish to adopt babies through your agency, one couple asks you how they should deal with the question of whether the child should be told that he is adopted.
Of the following, your BEST response to this couple is to
- A. tell them to conceal from the child the fact that he is adopted
- B. suggest that they lead the child to believe that his natural parents are dead
- C. tell them to inform the child that they know nothing about his natural parents
- D. explore with them their feelings about revealing to the child that he is adopted

6. You are beginning an investigation of an anonymous complaint that a welfare client has a concealed bank account.
Of the following, the FIRST step you should generally take in conducting this investigation is to
- A. confront the client with the complaint during an office interview
- B. try to track down the source of the anonymous complaint
- C. make a surprise visit to the client in his home to question him
- D. gather any available information from bank and agency records

7. When investigating the location of an absent parent, the worker frequently interviews the parent's friends and neighbors. The worker often writes down the information given by the person interviewed and, at the end of the interview, summarizes the information to the person.
For the worker to do this is, generally,
- A. *good practice*, because the person interviewed will be impressed by the efficiency of the worker
- B. *poor practice*, because the person interviewed may become impatient with the worker for repeating the information
- C. *good practice*, because the person interviewed has an opportunity to correct any errors the worker may have in recording the information
- D. *poor practice*, because summarizing the information may encourage the person to waste time adding and changing information

3 (#1)

8. During an interview for the purpose of investigating a charge of child abuse, a client first denied that she had abused her child, but then burst into tears and promised that she *will never do it again.*
   Of the following, the MOST appropriate action for the worker to take in this situation is to
   A. tell the client that, since she has already lied, it is difficult to believe that she will keep her promise
   B. show a concern for the client's feelings but tell her that you will have to report your findings and refer her for help
   C. determine the extent to which the child was abused and close the case if no permanent harm was done
   D. explain to the client that she has already done enough harm to the child and you must, therefore, recommend placement

8.____

9. As a worker involved in locating absent parents, you have obtained information indicating that the address for the putative father is the same as the client's address.
   In order to determine whether, in fact, the client and putative father are living together, of the following, it would be MOST appropriate to
   A. visit the address and question the neighbors and superintendent about the putative father
   B. visit the client to ask her why she has concealed the fact that the putative father is living with her
   C. file the information in the case folder and wait for confirming information
   D. close the client's case and issue a recoupment notice to the putative father

9.____

10. A client claims that she never received a welfare check that was due her. As part of your investigation of her claim, you obtain from the bank a copy of the check, which has been endorsed with her name and cashed.
    Of the following, the BEST procedure for you to follow in this investigation is to
    A. end the investigation immediately, since the client's claim cannot be proved
    B. interview the client and show her the copy of the cashed check
    C. tell the client that you have evidence that her claim is false
    D. say nothing about the cashed check and try to trap the client in a false statement

10.____

11. As part of the investigation to locate an absent father, you make a field visit to interview one of the father's friends. Before beginning the interview, you identify yourself to the friend and show him your official identification.
    For you to do this is, generally,
    A. *good practice,* because the friend will have proof that you are authorized to make such confidential investigations
    B. *poor practice,* because the friend may not answer your questions when he knows why you are interviewing him

11.____

3

C. *good practice*, because your supervisor can confirm from the friend that you actually made the interview
D. *poor practice*, because the friend may warn the absent father that your agency is looking for him

12. As a field office worker you are investigating a citizen's complaint charging a mother of three children with child neglect. The mother tells you that her husband has become depressed after losing his job and is often abusive to her, and that this situation has made her feel anxious and has made it difficult for her to care for the children properly.
Which one of the following is the BEST way for you to respond to this situation?
   A. Tell the mother that she must do everything possible to help her husband find a job
   B. Arrange to meet the husband so you can explain to him the consequences of his behavior
   C. Investigate the complaint, report your findings, and refer the family for counseling or other appropriate services
   D. Suggest that the family obtain homemaker services so that the mother can go to work

13. You are interviewing a client in his home as part of your investigation of an anonymous complaint that he has been receiving Medicaid fraudulently.
During the interview, the client frequently interrupts your questions to discuss the hardships of his life and the bitterness he feels about his medical condition.
Of the following, the BEST way for you to deal with these discussions is to
   A. cut them off abruptly, since the client is probably just trying to avoid answering your questions
   B. listen patiently, since these discussions may be helpful to the client and may give you information for your investigation
   C. remind the client that you are investigating a complaint against him and he must answer directly
   D. seek to gain the client's confidence by discussing any personal or medical problems which you yourself may have

14. While interviewing an absent father to determine his ability to pay child support, you realize that his answers to some of your questions contradict his answers to other questions.
Of the following, the BEST way for you to try to get accurate information from the father is to
   A. confront him with his contradictory answers and demand an explanation from him
   B. use your best judgment as to which of his answers are accurate and question him accordingly
   C. tell him that he has misunderstood your questions and that he must clarify his answers
   D. ask him the same questions in different words and follow up his answers with related questions

15. You are assigned to investigate a complaint of child neglect made against a minority mother by her non-minority neighbor. During an interview with you, the neighbor states that the mother allows her children to run around the streets half-dressed till late at night, and adds: *Of course, what can you expect from any of those people anyway?*
Your MOST appropriate action is to
- A. end the investigation, since the neighbor is clearly too prejudiced to be reliable
- B. tell the mother that the neighbor has made a complaint of child neglect against her
- C. seek evidence to support the complaint of child neglect made by the neighbor
- D. continue the interview with the neighbor in an attempt to get at the root of his prejudice against the mother

15.____

16. You are interviewing a couple with regard to available services for the husband's aged mother. During the interview, the husband casually mentions that he and his wife are thinking about becoming foster parents and would like to get some information on foster care programs offered through the Department of Social Services.
Of the following agencies within social services, the MOST appropriate one for you to refer this couple to is
- A. family and adult services
- B. special services for children
- C. bureau of child support
- D. special services for adults

16.____

17. You have been helping one of your clients to obtain medical assistance for her two young children. Accidentally, you obtain evidence that the client may be involved in a criminal scheme to collect duplicate welfare checks at several different addresses.
Of the following offices of the Department of Social Services, the MOST appropriate one to which you should report this evidence is
- A. the inspector general
- B. case intake and management
- C. the general counsel
- D. income support

17.____

Questions 18-25.

DIRECTIONS: Questions 18 through 25 are to be answered SOLELY on the basis of the Fact Situation and Report Form.

FACT SITUATION

On June 5, 2020, Mary Adams (Case No. 2095732), living at 1507 Montague Street, Apt. 3C, Brooklyn, New York, applied and was accepted for public assistance for herself and her three dependent children. Her husband, John, had left their home after an argument the previous week and had not returned, leaving Mrs. Adams without funds of any kind. She had tried to contact him at his place of employment, but was told that he had resigned several days prior to her call. When the case worker questioned Mrs. Adams about her husband's employment, income, and bank accounts, Mrs. Adams stated that he had done carpentry work during most of the years he had worked; his last known employer had been the Avco Lumber Company, 309 Amber Street, Queens, New York, where he had earned a weekly salary of $300. She then showed the case worker two bankbooks in her husband's name, which indicated a balance of $500 in one account and $275 in the other. A visit to Mr. Brown, a neighbor of the Adams', by the case worker, revealed that Mr. Adams had also told Mr. Brown about the existence of the bankbooks. A visit to the Avco Lumber Company by the case worker confirmed that Mr. Adams' gross salary had been $300 a week. This visit also revealed that Mr. Adams was a member of the Woodworkers' Union, Local #3, and that Mr. Adams' previous home address for the period February '09 to June '15 was 1109 Wellington Street, Brooklyn, New York.

```
                              REPORT FORM
A. CLIENT:
   1. Name:_____
   2. Address:_____
   3. Case No:_____
   4. Acceptance Date:_____
   5. No. of Dependent Children:_____
B. ABSENT PARENT:
   1. Name:_____
   2. Date of Birth:_____
   3. Place of Birth:_____
   4. Present Address:_____
   5. Regular Occupation:_____
   6. Union Affiliation:_____
   7. Name of Last Employer:_____
   8. Address of Last Employer:_____
   9. a. Weekly Earnings (Gross):_____
      b. How Verified:_____
  10. a. Weekly Earnings (Net):_____
      b. How Verified:_____
  11. a. Amount of Bank Accounts:_____
      b. How Verified:_____
  12. Social Security No.:_____
  13. Last Known Home Address:_____
  14. Previous Address:_____
```

18. Based on the information given in the Fact Situation, the MOST appropriate of the following entries for Item B.11.b is:
    A. Revealed to case worker by Mrs. Adams
    B. Confirmed by visit to Mr. Brown
    C. Revealed by Woodworkers' Union, Local #7
    D. Confirmed by bankbooks shown by Mrs. Adams

18.____

7 (#1)

19. The one of the following which BEST answers Item B.4 is
    A. Unknown
    B. c/o Avco Lumber Company
    C. 1109 Wellington Street, Brooklyn, New York
    D. 1507 Montague Street, Brooklyn, New York

    19.____

20. Based on the information given in the Fact Situation, it is NOT possible to answer Item
    A. A.2 B. A.5 C. B.6 D. B.10

    20.____

21. The one of the following which would be LEAST helpful in tracing the missing parent is information found in Item
    A. B.12 B. B.10.a C. B.6 D. B.1

    21.____

22. Based on the information given in the Fact Situation, it is MOST likely that the same entry would be made for Items
    A. A.1 and B.1
    B. A.4 and B.2
    C. B.9.a and B.10.a
    D. A.2 and B.13

    22.____

23. Based on the information in the Fact Situation, the entry: 1109 Wellington Street, Brooklyn, New York would MOST likely be placed for Item
    A. A.2 B. B.4 C. B.8 D. B.14

    23.____

24. The one of the following items that can be answered based on the information given in the Fact Situation is
    A. B.2 B. B.3 C. B.9.b D. B.12

    24.____

25. Based on the information given in the Fact Situation, the figure 775 would appear in the entry for
    A. A.3 B. B.12 C. B.9.a D. B.11.a

    25.____

KEY (CORRECT ANSWERS)

1.	B		11.	A
2.	C		12.	C
3.	C		13.	B
4.	B		14.	D
5.	D		15.	C
6.	D		16.	B
7.	C		17.	A
8.	B		18.	D
9.	A		19.	A
10.	B		20.	D

21.	B
22.	D
23.	D
24.	C
25.	D

TEST 2

DIRECTIONS: Each question or incomplete statement is followed by several suggested answers or completions. Select the one that BEST answers the question or completes the statement. *PRINT THE LETTER OF THE CORRECT ANSWER IN THE SPACE AT THE RIGHT.*

1. A worker in a senior adult center is approached by one of his clients, an elderly man living alone and suffering from severe arthritis, who asks him how to go about obtaining homemaker services through the Department of Social Services.
   Of the following, the MOST appropriate office of the department to which the worker should refer this client is
   A. income support
   B. protective services for adults
   C. income maintenance
   D. case intake and management

   1._____

2. Workers assigned to locate absent parents frequently ask various governmental agencies to search their records for information useful in determining the address of the person they are seeking.
   Of the following, which is likely to be useful MOST frequently for this purpose is the
   A. motor vehicle bureau
   B. office of the district attorney
   C. department of investigation
   D. health and hospitals corporation

   2._____

Questions 3-7.

DIRECTIONS: Questions 3 through 7 are to be answered SOLELY on the basis of the following Fact Situation and Preliminary Investigation Form.

FACT SITUATION

COMPLAINT:
On March 1, Mrs. Mona Willard, a neighbor of the Smith family, reported to the Police Department that the Smith children were being severely neglected, and she requested that an investigation be conducted. She based her complaint on the fact that, since the time three weeks ago when Janet Smith's husband, Charles, deserted Mrs. Smith and their two children, John, age 2, and Darlene, age 4, the children have been seen wandering in the neighborhood at all hours, inadequately dressed against the cold.

INVESTIGATION:
Investigation by the Police Department and the Department of Social Services revealed that the above charge was true and, further, that Mrs. Smith had inflicted cruel and harsh physical treatment upon the children in an attempt to discipline them. The children were immediately removed from their parent's care and placed in a medical facility for tests and observation. It was found that the children were suffering from serious malnutrition and anemia and that they also showed signs of emotional disturbance.

2 (#2)

CASE ACTION DECISION:
Conferences which you, the case worker, have held with Dr. Charles Jordan, a physician treating Mrs. Smith, and with Ellen Farraday, a psychiatric social worker from the Mental Health Consultation Center, confirm that Mrs. Smith is emotionally unstable at the present time and cannot care for her children. A written report from the Chief Resident Physician at the hospital where the children have been placed indicates that both children are presently doing well, but when released will need the security of an emotionally stable atmosphere. It has therefore been decided that placement in a foster home is necessary for the children until such time as Mrs. Smith is judged to be capable of caring for them.

PRELIMINARY INVESTIGATION FORM

1. Child(ren) in Need of Protection:
   a. Name(s): _____
   b. Age(s): _____
2. Alleged Perpetrator:
   a. Name _____
   b. Relationship _____
3. Present Status of Child(ren):
   ☐ a. Remaining with Subject Pending Investigation
   ☐ b. Removed to Relatives
   ☐ c. Removed to Foster Care
   ☐ d. In Hospital
   ☐ e. Other
4. Actions or Services Needed for Child(ren)
   ☐ a. Housekeeper
   ☐ b. Homemaker
   ☐ c. Day Care
   ☐ d. Home Attendant
   ☐ e. Relatives
   ☐ f. Foster Care
5. Contacts Made to Support Case Action Decision

	I Phone	II Personal	III Written
a. Medical; School	☐	☐	☐
b. Relatives	☐	☐	☐
c. Social Agency	☐	☐	☐
d. Other	☐	☐	☐

3. The one of the following that should be entered in space 2.b is   3.____
   A. mother   B. father   C. neighbor   D. physician

4. The one of the following boxes that should be checked in Item 3 is   4.____
   A. a   B. c   C. d   D. e

5. The one of the following boxes that should be checked in Item 4 is   5.____
   A. a   B. c   C. d   D. f

3 (#2)

6. Based on the information given in the Fact Situation, the boxes that should be checked off in Item 5 are:
   A. a-II, a-III, C-II
   B. a-II, c-II, c-III
   C. a-I, a-II, a-III
   D. b-II, c-I, c-II

7. The one of the following that would CORRECTLY appear as part of the entry

Questions 8-12.

DIRECTIONS: Questions 8 through 12 are to be answered SOLELY on the basis of the information contained in the following passage.

It is desirable, whenever possible, to have long-term elderly patients return to their own homes after hospitalization, provided that the medical condition is not acute. Of course, there must be room for the patient; the family must be able to provide some necessary care; and a physician's services must be available. Although the patient's family may be able to provide most services for the patient in his own home, this is generally unlikely because of the nature of the illness and the patient's need for a variety of services. Recently, hospital personnel, public health workers, visiting nurse associations, and community leaders have been developing home-care programs, which make the services of the hospital available to the patient who is not ill enough to require the concentrated technical facilities of a general hospital, but who is unable to attend an outpatient clinic or a physician's office. These services are those of the physician, visiting nurse, physical therapist, occupational therapist, social worker, and homemaker, as needed. There is also provision for readmission to the hospital for specific purposes and return to home care.

8. According to the above passage, it would be UNDESIRABLE to have an elderly patient return to his own home after hospitalization when the patient
   A. requires the services of doctor
   B. may be in immediate danger due to his medical condition
   C. is under physical or occupational therapy
   D. cannot go to the outpatient clinic of the hospital

9. According to the above passage, the *services of the hospital* which are made available by home-care programs include those of
   A. dietitians
   B. visiting nurses
   C. public health administers
   D. community workers

10. The one of the following statements about home-care programs which is BEST supported by the above paragraph is that home-care programs
    A. have been developed in part by hospital personnel
    B. relieve workloads of hospital personnel
    C. decrease public expenditures for hospitalization of the elderly
    D. reduce readmissions of elderly patients to hospitals

11. According to the above passage, home-care programs would be LEAST likely to include the services of a
    A. homemaker
    B. social worker
    C. physician
    D. hospital technician

11

12. It may be inferred from the above passage that a MAJOR purpose of home-care programs is to 12.____
    A. increase the demand for physicians, nurses, and other medical personnel
    B. provide patients in their homes with services similar to those provided in hospitals
    C. reduce the need for general hospitals and outpatient clinics
    D. relieve the family of their responsibility of caring for the patient

Questions 13-17.

DIRECTIONS: Questions 13 through 17 are to be answered SOLELY on the basis of the information contained in the following Duties Statement.

DUTIES STATEMENT OF THE VIOLATION CENTER (VC) CASE WORKER

1. Receives telephone, mail, and in-person reports of suspected violations from mandated and non-mandated sources, as well as from the New York State Violation Bureau (NYSVB), on form DSS-555, within 48 hours, to the Central Office of VC, 265 Church Street, New York, N.Y.

2. Completes in-office portion of DSS-555 received from mandated sources as fully as possible. Checks that report summary is specific, factual, and detailed. (See NYSVB instructions on Page 213)

3. When DSS-555 is received, clears Central Office of VC for any previous record of violation on file in Central Office. If record exists, enters additional information from file record on to DSS-555. Also requests Central Office Clerk to provide appropriate record number of previous record and enters additional information from file record on to DSS-555. Also requests Central Office Clerk to provide appropriate record number of previous record and enters it in correct box on form.

4. Determines appropriate Central Office Sex Code and Reporting Source Code for each violation. (The Codes are in the VC Manual.) The codes are then entered on the bottom of the reverse side of the DSS-555.

5. Determines appropriate Service Area Code for the address in the summary. The address is the location of the violation, if known. (If the location of the violation is unknown, the address of the primary witness shall be used.) Enters Service Area Code on reverse of DSS-555. All report summaries involving violations by N.Y.C. employees are sent to the Manhattan Borough Office of VC for clearance and transmittal to BEM.

---

13. According to the above Duties Statement, when a report of a suspected violation is received, a written summary of their report on DSS-555 must be sent within 48 hours by 13.____
    A. mandated sources
    B. non-mandated sources
    C. the NYSVB
    D. mandated and non-mandated sources, as well as by the NYSVB

5 (#2)

14. From the above Duties Statement, it may be *inferred* that the case worker whose duties are described is MOST likely assigned to
    A. the Manhattan Borough Office of VC
    B. the New York State Violation Bureau
    C. the Central Office of VC
    D. BEM

14.____

15. According to the above Duties Statement, the Central Office Sex Code is entered on the DSS-555
    A. on the opposite side from the Service Area Code
    B. on the front of the form
    C. above the Service Area Code on the form
    D. on the bottom of the back of the form

15.____

16. According to the above Duties Statement, a case worker can determine the appropriate Reporting Source Code for a violation by consulting
    A. NYSVB Instructions
    B. the Central Office Clerk
    C. the VC Manual
    D. the Service Area Code

16.____

17. As used in paragraph 2 of the above Duties Statement, the word *detailed* means MOST NEARLY
    A. full descriptive
    B. complicated
    C. of considerable length
    D. well-written

17.____

Questions 18-25.

DIRECTIONS: Questions 18 through 25 are to be answered SOLELY on the basis of the following Semi-Monthly Family Allowance Schedule for Maintenance of Legally Responsible Relative (Figure No. 1) and Conversion Table (Figure 2) given on the following pages and the information and case situations given below).

FIGURE NO. 1

SEMI-MONTHLY FAMILY ALLOWANCE SCHEDULE FOR MAINTENANCE OF LEGALLY RESPONSIBLE RELATIVE AND DEPENDENTS BASED UPON TOTAL NUMBER OF PERSONS IN PRESENT HOUSEHOLD. (ALL SURPLUS IS TO BE USED AS CONTRIBUTION TO RECIPIENTS OF PUBLIC ASSISTANCE.)

TOTAL NUMBER OF PERSONS IN PRESENT HOUSEHOLD	ONE	TWO	THREE	FOUR	FIVE	SIX	EACH ADDITIONAL PERSON
SEMI-MONTHLY FAMILY ALLOWANCE	$1,600	$1,915	$2,200	$2,605	$2,800	$3,205	$350

FIGURE NO. 2
CONVERSION TABLE – WEEKLY TO SEMI-MONTHLY AMOUNTS

DOLLARS				CENTS			
Weekly Amount	Semi-Monthly Amount	Weekly Amount	Semi-Monthly Amount	Weekly Amount	Semi-Monthly Amount	Weekly Amount	Semi-Monthly Amount
$10	$21.70	$510.00	$1105.00	$0.10	$0.20	$5.10	$11.10
20.00	86.70	520.00	1126.70	0.20	0.40	5.20	11.30
30.00	65.00	530.00	1148.30	0.30	0.70	5.30	11.50
40.00	86.70	540.00	1170.00	0.40	0.90	5.40	11.70
50.00	108.30	550.00	1191.70	0.50	1.10	5.50	11.90
60.00	130.00	560.00	1213.30	0.60	1.30	5.60	12.10
70.00	151.70	570.00	1235.00	0.70	1.50	5.70	12.40
80.00	173.30	580.00	1256.70	1.00	1.70	5.80	12.60
90.00	195.00	590.00	1278.30	0.90	2.00	5.90	12.80
100.00	216.70	600.00	1300.00	1.00	2.20	6.00	13.00
110.00	238.30	610.00	1321.70	1.10	2.40	6.10	13.20
120.00	260.00	620.00	1343.30	1.20	2.60	6.20	13.40
130.00	281.70	630.00	1365.00	1.30	2.80	6.30	13.70
140.00	303.30	640.00	1386.70	1.40	3.00	6.40	13.90
150.00	325.00	650.00	1408.30	1.50	3.30	6.50	14.10
160.00	346.70	660.00	1430.00	1.60	3.50	6.60	14.30
170.00	368.30	670.00	1451.40	1.70	3.70	6.70	14.50
180.00	390.00	680.00	1473.30	1.80	3.90	6.80	14.70
190.00	411.70	690.00	1495.00	1.90	4.10	6.90	15.00
200.00	433.30	700.00	1516.70	2.00	4.30	7.00	15.20
210.00	455.00	710.00	1538.30	2.10	4.60	7.10	15.40
220.00	476.70	720.00	1560.00	2.20	4.80	7.20	15.60
230.00	498.30	730.00	1581.70	2.30	5.00	7.30	15.80
240.00	520.00	740.00	1603.30	2.40	5.20	7.40	16.00
250.00	541.70	750.00	1625.00	2.50	5.40	7.50	16.30
260.00	563.30	760.00	1646.70	2.60	5.60	7.60	16.50
270.00	585.00	770.00	1668.30	2.70	5.90	7.70	16.70
280.00	606.70	780.00	690.00	2.80	6.10	7.80	16.90
290.00	628.30	790.00	1711.70	2.90	6.30	7.90	17.10
300.00	650.00	800.00	1733.30	3.00	6.50	8.00	17.30
310.00	671.70	810.00	1755.00	3.10	6.70	8.10	17.60
320.00	693.30	820.00	1776.70	3.20	6.90	8.20	17.80
330.00	715.00	830.00	1798.30	3.30	7.20	8.30	18.00
340.00	736.70	840.00	1820.00	3.40	7.40	8.40	18.20
350.00	783.00	850.00	1841.70	3.50	7.60	8.50	18.40
360.00	780.00	860.00	1863.30	3.60	7.80	8.60	18.60
370.00	801.70	870.00	1885.00	3.70	8.00	8.70	18.90
380.00	823.30	880.00	1906.70	3.80	8.20	8.80	19.10
390.00	845.00	890.00	1928.30	3.90	8.50	8.90	19.30
400.00	866.70	900.00	1950.00	4.00	8.70	9.00	19.50
410.00	888.30	910.00	1971.70	4.10	8.90	9.10	19.70
420.00	910.00	920.00	1993.30	4.20	9.10	9.20	19.90
430.00	931.70	930.00	2015.00	4.30	9.30	9.30	20.20
440.00	953.30	940.00	2036.70	40.40	9.50	9.40	20.40
450.00	975.00	950.00	2058.30	40.50	9.80	9.50	20.60
460.00	996.70	960.00	2080.00	4.60	10.00	9.60	20.80
470.00	1018.30	970.00	2101.70	4.70	10.20	9.70	21.00
480.00	1040.00	980.00	2123.30	4.80	10.40	9.80	21.20
490.00	1061.70	990.00	2145.00	4.90	10.60	9.90	21.50
500.00	1083.30	1000.00	2166.70	5.00	10.80		

7 (#2)

INFORMATION

Legally responsible relatives living apart from persons on public assistance are asked to contribute toward the support of these persons. The amount of contribution depends on several factors, such as the number of persons in the legally responsible relative's present household who are dependent on his income (including himself), the amount of his gross income, and his expenses incident to employment. Since his contribution is computed on a semi-monthly basis, all figures must be broken down into semi-monthly amounts. Weekly amounts can be converted into semi-monthly amounts by using the conversion table on page 6.

The amount of supported is computed as follows:

1. Determine total weekly gross income (the wages or salary before payroll deductions) of legally responsible relative.
2. Deduct all weekly expenses incident to employment such as federal, state, and city income taxes, Social Security payments, State Disability Insurance payments, union dues, cost of transportation, and $10.00 maximum per work day for lunch.
3. Remaining income shall be considered as weekly net income of legally responsible relative.
4. Convert weekly net income to semi-monthly net income, using data in Figure No. 2.
5. Semi-monthly net income is compared to the semi-monthly allowance (see Figure No. 1). If there is an excess of net income, then that amount is considered available as the contribution to the public assistance household. If the semi-monthly allowance is greater than the semi-monthly net income, then there is an income deficit, and there is no income available as a contribution to the public assistance household.
6. The formula for computing the semi-monthly contribution is:
Semi-Monthly Net Income • Semi-Monthly Family Allowance = Semi-Monthly Amount of Income Available Towards Contribution to Public Assistance Household

Case Situation No. 1:

Mr. Andrew Young is separated from his wife and family and lives with one dependent in a 3-room furnished apartment. Mr. Young is employed as a dishwasher and his gross wages are $1,000 per week. He is employed 5 days a week and spends $14.40 a day for carfare. He spends $20.00 a work day on lunch. His weekly salary deductions are as follows:

Federal Income Tax	$142.30
State Income Tax	26.00
City Income Tax	9.80
Social Security	62.10
New York State Disability Insurance	5.30
Union Due	5.00

Mr. Young's wife and two children, for whom he is legally responsible, are currently receiving public assistance.

8 (#2)

18. The weekly amount that Mr. Young contributes toward Social Security, New York State Disability Insurance, Income Taxes, and Union Dues is MOST NEARLY
    A. $214.70   B. $250.50   C. $320.50   D. $370.50

18.____

19. The total amount of all weekly expenses incident to Mr. Young's employment which should be deducted from his weekly gross earnings is MOST NEARLY
    A. $214.70   B. $250.50   C. $370.50   D. $420.50

19.____

20. Which one of the following amounts is Mr. Young's semi-monthly net income?
    A. $1259.00   B. $1363.90   C. $1623.90   D. $1701.50

20.____

21. The semi-monthly amount of income available to the contribution to Mr. Young's wife and two children is MOST NEARLY
    A. $0.00   B. $23.90   C. $236.10   D. $551.10

21.____

Case Situation No. 2:

Mr. Donald Wilson resides with six dependents in a seven-room unfurnished apartment. Mr. Wilson is employed as an automobile salesman and his gross wages are $4,000 per week. He is employed five days a week and spends $10.00 a day carfare. He spends $50.00 a work day for lunch. His weekly salary deductions are as follows:

Federal Income Tax	$$705.50
State Income Tax	150.00
City Income Tax	97.00
Social Security	301.00
New York State Disability Insurance	52.50
Union Due	Not Union Member

22. The weekly amount that Mr. Wilson contributes toward Social Security, New York State Disability Insurance, Federal Income Tax, and Union Dues is MOST NEARLY
    A. $1059.00   B. $1159.00   C. $1306.00   D. $1406.00

22.____

23. The total amount of all weekly expenses incident to Mr. Wilson's employment, which should be deducted from his weekly gross earnings is MOST NEARLY
    A. $1159.00   B. $1306.00   C. $1406.00   D. $1606.00

23.____

24. The semi-monthly family allowance for Mr. Wilson and his six dependents is MOST NEARLY
    A. $2594.00   B. $3205.00   C. $1406.00   D. $4000.00

24.____

25. The semi-monthly amount Mr. Wilson's income available for contribution to his wife and child is MOST NEARLY
    A. $1633.00   B. $2065.40   C. $2594.00   D. $2810.20

25.____

KEY (CORRECT ANSWERS)

1.	D		11.	D
2.	A		12.	B
3.	A		13.	A
4.	C		14.	C
5.	D		15.	D
6.	A		16.	C
7.	C		17.	A
8.	B		18.	B
9.	B		19.	C
10.	A		20.	B

21. A
22. A
23. C
24. C
25. B

EXAMINATION SECTION
TEST 1

DIRECTIONS: Each question or incomplete statement is followed by several suggested answers or completions. Select the one that BEST answers the question or completes the statement. *PRINT THE LETTER OF THE CORRECT ANSWER IN THE SPACE AT THE RIGHT.*

1. The PRIMARY function of the Department of Social Services is to
    A. refer needy persons to legally responsible relatives for support
    B. enable needy persons to become self-supporting
    C. refer ineligible persons to private agencies
    D. grant aid to needy eligible persons
    E. administer public assistance programs in which the federal and state governments do not participate

1.____

2. A public assistance program objective should be designed to
    A. provide for eligible persons in accordance with their individual requirements and with consideration of the circumstances in which they live
    B. provide for eligible persons at a standard of living equal to that enjoyed while they were self-supporting
    C. make sure that assistance payments from public funds are not too liberal
    D. guard against providing a better living for persons receiving aid than is enjoyed by the most frugal independent families
    E. eliminate the need for private welfare agencies

2.____

3. It is often stated that it would be better to abolish the need for relief rather than to extend the existing public assistance programs.
   This statement suggests that
    A. existing legislation makes it too easy for people to apply for and receive assistance
    B. public assistance should be limited to institutional care for rehabilitative purposes
    C. the support of needy persons should be the responsibility of their own families and relatives rather than that of the government
    D. the existing criteria used to determine *need* for public assistance are too liberal and should be modified to include a *work* test
    E. attempts should be made to eradicate those forces in our social organization which cause poverty

3.____

4. The one of the following types of public assistance which is frequently described as a *special privilege* is
    A. veteran assistance
    B. emergency assistance
    C. aid to dependent children
    D. old-age assistance
    E. vocational rehabilitation of the handicapped

4.____

5. The principle of *settlement* holds that each community is responsible for the care of its own members and that communities should not bear the costs of care for needy non-residents.
   This was an intrinsic principle of the
   - A. English Poor Laws
   - B. Home Rule Amendment
   - C. Single Tax Proposal
   - D. National Bankruptcy Regulations
   - E. Proportional Representation Act

   5.____

6. The FIRST form of state social security legislation developed in the United States was
   - A. health insurance
   - B. unemployment compensation
   - C. workmen's compensation
   - D. old-age insurance
   - E. old-age assistance

   6.____

7. The plan for establishing a federal department with Cabinet status to be known as the Department of Health, Education, and Welfare, was
   - A. vetoed by the President after having been passed by Congress
   - B. disapproved by the Senate after having been passed by the House of Representatives
   - C. rejected by both the Senate and the House of Representatives
   - D. enacted into legislation during a past session of Congress
   - E. determined to be unconstitutional

   7.____

8. Census Bureau reports show certain definite social trends in our population. One of these trends which was a major contributing factor in the establishment of the federal old-age insurance system was the
   - A. increased rate of immigration to the United States
   - B. rate at which the number of Americans living to 65 years of age and beyond is increasing
   - C. increasing amounts spent for categorical relief in the country as a whole
   - D. decreasing number of legally responsible relatives who have been unable to assist the aged since the Depression of 1929
   - E. number of states which have failed to meet their obligations in the care of the aged

   8.____

9. The Federal Housing Administration is the agency which
   - A. insures mortgages made by lending institutions for new construction or remodeling of old construction
   - B. provides federal aid for state and local governments for slum clearance and housing for very low income families
   - C. subsidizes the building industry through direct grants
   - D. provides for the construction of low-cost housing projects owned and operated by the federal government
   - E. combines city planning with government subsidies for large-scale housing

   9.____

10. Reports show that more men than women are physically handicapped MAINLY because
    A. women are instinctively more cautious than men
    B. men are more likely to have congenital deformities
    C. women tend to see surgical remedies because of greater concern over personal appearance
    D. men have lower ability to recover from injury
    E. men are more likely to be exposed to hazardous conditions

    10.____

11. Of the following, the explanation married women give MOST frequently for seeking employment outside the home is that they wish to
    A. escape the drudgeries of home life
    B. develop secondary employment skills
    C. maintain an emotionally satisfying career
    D. provide the main support for the family
    E. supplement the family income

    11.____

12. Of the following home conditions, the one MOST likely to cause emotional disturbances in children is
    A. increased birthrate following the war
    B. disrupted family relationships
    C. lower family income than that of neighbors
    D. higher family income than that of neighbors
    E. overcrowded living conditions

    12.____

13. Casual unemployment, as distinguished from other types of unemployment, is traceable MOST readily to
    A. a decrease in the demand for labor as a result of scientific progress
    B. more or less haphazard changes in the demand for labor in certain industries
    C. periodic changes in the demand for labor in certain industries
    D. disturbances and disruptions in industry resulting from international trade barriers
    E. increased mobility of the population

    13.____

14. Labor legislation, although primarily intended for the benefit of the employee, may aid the employer by
    A. increasing his control over the immediate labor market
    B. prohibiting government interference with operating policies
    C. protecting him, through equalization of labor costs, from being undercut by other employers
    D. transferring to the general taxpayer the principal costs of industrial hazards of accident and unemployment
    E. increasing the pensions of civil service employees

    14.____

15. When employment and unemployment figures both decline, the MOST probable conclusion is that
    A. the population has reached a condition of equilibrium
    B. seasonal employment has ended

    15.____

C. the labor force has decreased
D. payments for unemployment insurance have been increased
E. industrial progress has reduced working hours

16. In evaluating the adequacy of an individual's income, a social service worker should place primary emphasis on
    A. its value in relation to the average income
    B. the source of the income
    C. its relation to the earning capacity of the individual
    D. its purchasing power
    E. the purposes for which it is spent

16.____

17. An individual with an I.Q. of 100 may be said to have demonstrated _____ intelligence.
    A. superior
    B. absolute
    C. substandard
    D. approximately average
    E. high average

17.____

18. While state legislatures differ in many respects, all of them are MOST NEARLY alike in
    A. provisions for retirement of members
    B. rate of pay
    C. length of legislative sessions
    D. method of selection of their members
    E. length of term of office

18.____

19. If a state passed a law in a field under Congressional jurisdiction and if Congress subsequently passed contrary legislation, the state provision would be
    A. regarded as never having existed
    B. valid until the next session of the state legislature which would be obliged to repeal it
    C. superseded by the federal statute
    D. ratified by Congress
    E. still operative in the state involved

19.____

20. Power to pardon offenses committed against the people of the United States is vested in the
    A. Supreme Court of the United States
    B. United States District Courts
    C. Federal Bureau of Investigation
    D. United States Parole Board
    E. President of the United States

20.____

21. As distinguished from formal social control of an individual's behavior, an example of informal social control is that exerted by
    A. public opinion
    B. religious doctrine
    C. educational institutions
    D. statutes
    E. public health measures

21.____

5 (#1)

22. The PRINCIPAL function of the jury in a jury trial is to decide questions of 22._____
    A. equity   B. fact   C. injunction
    D. contract   D. law

23. Of the following rights of an individual, the one which usually depends on citizenship as distinguished from those given anyone living under the laws of the United States is the right to 23._____
    A. receive public assistance
    B. hold an elective office
    C. petition the government for redress of grievances
    D. receive equal protection of the laws
    E. be accorded a trial by jury

24. The name of Thomas Malthus is MOST closely associated with a work on 24._____
    A. population   B. political justice   C. capitalism
    D. social contract   E. wealth of nations

25. A chronic functional disease characterized by fits or attacks in which there is a loss of consciousness with a succession of convulsions is called 25._____
    A. epilepsy   B. dipsomania   C. catalepsy
    D. Hodgkin's disease   E. paresis

KEY (CORRECT ANSWERS)

1.	D		11.	E
2.	A		12.	B
3.	E		13.	B
4.	A		14.	C
5.	A		15.	C
6.	C		16.	D
7.	D		17.	D
8.	B		18.	D
9.	A		19.	C
10.	E		20.	E

21. A
22. B
23. B
24. A
25. A

TEST 2

DIRECTIONS: Each question or incomplete statement is followed by several suggested answers or completions. Select the one that BEST answers the question or completes the statement. *PRINT THE LETTER OF THE CORRECT ANSWER IN THE SPACE AT THE RIGHT.*

Questions 1-10.

DIRECTIONS: Questions 1 through 10, inclusive, are based on the following table, which gives a partial summary of certain groups of cases in the social services center of a public assistance agency.

SOCIAL SERVICES CENTER CASELOAD SUMMARY, JUNE-SEPTEMBER

	June	July	August	September
Total Cases Under Care at End of Month	13,790	11,445	13,191	12,209
Home relief	4,739	2,512	6,055	5,118
Old-age assistance	5,337	b	5,440	2,265
Aid to dependent children	3,487	1,621	1,520	4,594
Aid to the Blind	227	251	176	232
Net Change During Month	-344	c	1,746	-982
Applications Made During Month	1,542	789	3,153	1,791
Total Cases Accepted during Month	534	534	2,879	982
Home relief	278	213	342	338
Old-age assistance	43	161	1,409	f
Aid to dependent children	195	153	1,115	307
Aid to the blind	18	7	13	14
Total Cases Closed During Month	878	d	1,133	1,964
To private employment	326	1,197	460	870
To unemployment insurance	96	421	126	205
Reclassified	176	326	178	399
All other reasons	280	935	e	490
Total Cases Carried Over to Next Month	a	11,445	13,191	12,209

1. The number which should be placed in the blank indicated by *a* is
    A. 12,912   B. 13,446   C. 13,790
    D. 14,134   E. None of the above

    1._____

2. The number which should be placed in the blank indicated by *b* is
    A. 6,385   B. 7,601   C. 8,933
    D. 7,061   E. None of the above

    2._____

3. The number which should be placed in the blank indicated by *c* is
    A. -2,345   B. -344   C. 344
    D. 3,413   E. None of the above

    3._____

2 (#2)

4. The number which should be placed in the blank indicated by *d* is
   A. 2,789 B. 2,345 C. 7,601
   D. 3,879 E. None of the above

   4.____

5. Of the total number of cases closed during the month of August, the percentage closed for reasons other than reclassification or receipt of unemployment insurance is APPROXIMATELY
   A. 13.8% B. 73.17% C. 26.83% D. 40.60% E. 24.63%

   5.____

6. In comparing June and July, the figures indicate that with respect to the total cases under care at the end of each month,
   A. the percentage of total cases accepted during the month was lower in June
   B. the percentage of total cases accepted during the month was higher in June
   C. the percentage of total cases accepted during both months was the same
   D. there were more cases under care at the end of July
   E. there is insufficient data for comparison of the total cases under care at the end of each month

   6.____

7. The total number of cases accepted during the entire period in the category in which most cases were accepted was
   A. 1,409 B. 1,936 C. 1,770 D. 4,929 E. 20,103

   7.____

8. In comparing July and September, the figures indicate that
   A. more cases were closed in September because of private employment
   B. the total number of cases accepted during the month consisted of a greater proportion of home relief cases in September
   C. in one of these months, there were more total cases under care at the end of the month than at the beginning of the month
   D. aid to dependent children cases at the beginning of September numbered almost three times as many as at the beginning of July
   E. none of the above is correct

   8.____

9. The total number of applications made during the four-month period was
   A. more than four times the number of cases closed because of private employment during the same period
   B. less than the combined totals of aid to dependent children cases under care in June and July
   C. 4,376 more than the total number of cases accepted during August
   D. 23 times as large as the number of cases reclassified in July
   E. 5,916 less than the total number of cases carried over to September

   9.____

10. The ratio of old-age assistance cases accepted in August to the total number of such cases under care at the end of that month is expressed with the GREATEST degree of accuracy by the figures
    A. 1:4 B. 1:25 C. 4:1 D. 7:128 E. 10:39

    10.____

11. The term *mores* refers to
    A. English meadows   B. bribery   C. Moorish worship
    D. telegraphic code   E. social customs

12. *Disparity* refers MOST directly to
    A. difference   B. argument   C. low wages
    D. separation   E. injustice

13. The technical term used to express the ratio between mental and chronological age is called the
    A. mentality rating
    B. culture level index
    C. psychometric standard
    D. achievement index
    E. intelligence quotient

14. In social services work, the disorganizing factors in a personal or familial situation which prevent or hinder rehabilitation are called
    A. median deviations
    B. transference situations
    C. rank correlations
    D. liabilities
    E. collective representations

15. The period in the life of man when mental abilities begin to deteriorate is known as
    A. puberty   B. adolescence   C. gerontology
    D. senility   E. antiquity

Questions 16-25.

DIRECTIONS: Questions 16 through 25, inclusive, contain two blank spaces each. You are to select the words which will fill the blanks so that the sentence will be true and sensible. For the *first* blank in each question, select a word or phrase preceded by letter A, B, C, D, or E. For the *second* blank in the question, select a word or phrase preceded by letter V, W, X, Y, or Z. Use the two letters you have selected as your answer and print both these letters in the correspondingly numbered space at the right.

16. _____ is to public assistance as citizenship is to _____.
    A. need   B. school attendance   C. worthiness
    D. child   E. welfare center
    V. passport   W. alien   X. immigration
    Y. excise tax   Z. indictment

17. _____ is to home relief as public institutional care is to _____.
    A. compensation   B. supplementation
    C. direct relief   D. survivor's insurance
    E. fiscal period
    V. removal of custody   W. adoption
    X. indoor relief   Y. day care
    Z. voucher assistance

4 (#2)

18. _____ is to face sheet as income is to _____. 18._____
   A. client   B. cash relief
   C. relief standard   D. case record
   E. emergency assistance
   V. wages   W. home
   X. debts   Y. taxes
   Z. bonus

19. _____ is to demography as man is to _____. 19._____
   A. politics   B. racial relations   C. stigmata
   D. social statistics   E. democracy
   V. population   W. geography   X. woman
   Y. marriage   Z. anthropology

20. _____ is to tuberculosis as Terman is to_____. 20._____
   A. Wasserman   B. Mantoux   C. Schick
   D. Ascheim-Zondek   E. Snellen
   V. litmus test   W. means test   X. lie detector test
   Y. intelligence test   Z. CAVD test

21. _____ is to dementia as feeblemindedness is to _____. 21._____
   A. anger   B. luxation   C. insanity
   D. diagnosis   E. psychiatry
   V. myopia   W. amentia   X. tibia
   Y. criminal   Z. childhood

22. Frustration is to _____ as _____ is to relaxation. 22._____
   A. satisfaction   B. goal   C. need
   D. desire   E. motive
   V. tension   W. behavior   X. adjustment
   Y. readjustment   Z. reaction

23. _____ is to embezzlement as parole is to _____. 23._____
   A. intent   B. larceny   C. desertion
   D. guilt   E. conviction
   V. bail   W. plea   X. probation
   Y. innocence   Z. reformatory

24. Abandonment is to _____ as coercion is to _____. 24._____
   A. abduction   B. discovery   C. guardian
   D. adultery   E. desertion
   V. desertion   W. impotence   X. crime
   Y. coition   Z. constraint

25. _____ is to homicide as felony is to _____. 25._____
   A. courthouse   B. mayhem   C. negligence
   D. witness   E. manslaughter
   V. judge   W. crime   X. autopsy
   Y. civil suit   Z. prosecutor

KEY (CORRECT ANSWERS)

1. C
2. D
3. A
4. E
5. B

6. A
7. B
8. E
9. E
10. E

11. E
12. A
13. E
14. D
15. D

16. AV
17. CX
18. DV
19. DZ
20. BY

21. CW
22. AV
23. BX
24. EZ
25. EW

TEST 3

DIRECTIONS: Each question or incomplete statement is followed by several suggested answers or completions. Select the one that BEST answers the question or completes the statement. *PRINT THE LETTER OF THE CORRECT ANSWER IN THE SPACE AT THE RIGHT.*

Questions 1-3.

DIRECTIONS: Questions 1 through 3, inclusive, are to be answered on the basis of the following passage.

Aid to dependent children shall be given to a parent or other relative as herein specified for the benefit of a child or children under sixteen years of age or of a minor or minors between sixteen and eighteen years of age if in the judgment of the administrative agency: (1) the granting of an allowance will be in the interest of such child or minor, and (2) the parent or other relative is a fit person to bring up such child or minor so that his physical, mental, and moral well-being will be safeguarded, and (3) aid is necessary to enable such parent or other relative to do so, and (4) such child or minor is a resident of the state on the date of application for aid, and (5) such minor between sixteen and eighteen years of age is regularly attending school in accordance with the regulations of the department. An allowance may be granted for the aid of such child or minor who has been deprived or parental support or care by reason of the death, continued absence from the home, or physical or mental incapacity of a parent, and who is living with his father, mother, grandfather, grandmother, brother, sister, stepfather, stepmother, stepbrother, stepsister, uncle or aunt. In making such allowances, consideration shall be given to the ability of the relative making application and of any other relatives to support and care for or to contribute to the support and care of such child or minor. In making all such allowances, it shall be made certain that the religious faith of the child or minor shall be preserved and protected.

1. The preceding passage is concerned PRIMARILY with
    A. the financial ability of persons applying for public assistance
    B. compliance on the part of applicants with the *settlement* provisions of the law
    C. the fitness of parents or other relatives to bring up physically, mentally, or morally delinquent children between the ages of sixteen and eighteen
    D. eligibility for aid to dependent children
    E. the religious faith of children or minors coming within the provisions of this law

2. On the basis of the preceding passage, the MOST accurate of the following statements is:
    A. Mary Doe, mother of John, age 18, is entitled to aid for her son if he is attending school regularly
    B. Evelyn Stowe, mother of Eleanor, age 13, is not entitled to aid for Eleanor if she uses her home for immoral purposes
    C. Ann Roe, cousin of Helen, age 14, is entitled to aid for Helen if the latter is living with her
    D. Peter Moe, uncle of Henry, age 15, is not entitled to aid for Henry if the latter is living with him

1.____

2.____

29

E. Harriet Hoe, mother of Paul, age 7, is not entitled to aid for him if she has been divorced from her husband

3. The above passage is PROBABLY an excerpt of the
   A. Administrative Code
   B. Social Welfare Law
   C. Federal Security Act
   D. City Charter
   E. Colonial Laws of the state

4. Recent amendment of the Social Security Act has produced major changes in the administration of public assistance.
   The one of the following which is NOT included among these changes is the
   A. availability of federal funds in matching payments for home relief to veterans who are employable but unemployed
   B. establishment of federal grants-in-aid for a category of assistance to be known as aid to the permanently and totally disabled
   C. extension of the four categories of assistance to Puerto Rico and the Virgin Islands
   D. sharing by the federal government of costs of assistance to needy aged and blind persons in public medical institutions
   E. availability of federal funds within present federal maxima in matching indirect payments for medical care in old-age assistance, aid to the blind, and aid to dependent children

5. The length of residence required to make a person eligible for the various forms of public assistance available in the United States
   A. is the same in all states but is different among public assistance programs in a given state
   B. is the same in all states and among different public assistance programs in a given state
   C. is the same in all states for different categories
   D. varies among states and among different public assistance programs in a given state
   E. varies only in the local agencies of a given state

6. The Social Welfare Law requires that whenever an applicant for aid to dependent children resides in a place where there is a central index or a social service exchange, the public welfare official shall register the case with such index or exchange.
   This requirement is for the purpose of
   A. preventing duplication and coordinating the work of public and private agencies
   B. establishing prior claims on the amounts of assistance furnished when repayments are made
   C. having the social service exchange determine which agency should handle the case
   D. providing statistical data regarding the number of persons receiving grants for aid to dependent children
   E. making sure that opportunities for private employment are available to persons receiving assistance

3 (#3)

7. A person who knowingly brings a needy person from another state into the state for the purpose of making him a public charge, is guilty of
    A. violation of the Displaced Persons Act
    B. violation of the Mann Act
    C. a felony
    D. a misdemeanor
    E. no offense

7._____

8. Among the following needy persons, the one NOT eligible to receive veteran assistance is the
    A. husband of a veteran, if living with the veteran
    B. minor grandchild of a veteran, if living with the veteran
    C. incapacitated child of a deceased veteran
    D. stepmother of stepfather of a veteran, if living with the veteran
    E. non-veteran brother or sister of a veteran, if living with the veteran

8._____

9. The term *state residence*, as defined in the Social Welfare Law, means continuous residence within the state for a period of AT LEAST
    A. one year   B. two years   C. six months
    D. one month   E. one day

9._____

10. In order to be eligible for old-age assistance in this state, applicants must have resided continuously in the state prior to the date of application for
    A. three months   B. six months   C. one year
    D. five years   E. no specific period

10._____

11. Under the Social Security Act, public assistance payments do NOT provide for
    A. old-age assistance
    B. care of children in foster homes
    C. aid to the blind
    D. aid to dependent children
    E. aid to the permanently and totally disabled

11._____

12. The Social Welfare Law provides that certain relatives of a recipient of public assistance or care, or of a person liable to become in need thereof, be responsible for the support of such person if they are of sufficient ability. The one of the following who is NOT a legally responsible relative is a(n)
    A. mother
    B. child
    C. grandparent
    D. uncle
    E. step-parent, for a minor stepchild

12._____

13. Of the following, the distinguishing characteristics of a *dependent child* as defined in the Social Welfare Law, refer to a child who is
    A. in the custody of, or wholly or partly maintained by an authorized organization of charitable, eleemosynary, correctional, or reformatory character

13._____

B. in such condition of want or suffering or who under improper guardianship as to injure or endanger the morals of himself or others
C. between 16 and 18 years of age and solely dependent upon his parents for support and maintenance
D. under 16 years of age and deserted or abandoned by parents or other persons lawfully charged with his care
E. incorrigible or ungovernable and beyond the control of his parents or guardian

14. Recent adoption laws tend to place increased emphasis upon
    A. informal signing of adoption papers
    B. lowered residence requirements for adoption
    C. establishment of the child's inheritance rights
    D. social investigation of the home before adoption
    E. increased boarding rates paid to adoptive parents

14.____

15. Any person or organization soliciting donations in public places is required to have a license issued by the
    A. Police Department
    B. Department of Sanitation
    C. Division of Labor Relations
    D. Department of Social Services
    E. Department of Licenses

15.____

16. A person who, though himself, in good health, harbors disease germs which may be passed on to others, is called a(n)
    A. instigator
    B. carrier
    C. incubator
    D. inoculator
    E. malingerer

16.____

17. Diseases most commonly caused by certain working environments or conditions are known as _____ diseases.
    A. infectious
    B. contagious
    C. occupational
    D. hereditary
    E. compensatory

17.____

18. The process of destroying micro-organisms which cause disease or infection is called
    A. contamination
    B. immunization
    C. inoculation
    D. sterilization
    E. infestation

18.____

19. Proper utilization of the term *carious* would involve reference to
    A. teeth
    B. curiosity
    C. shipment of food packages to needy persons in Europe
    D. hazardous or precarious situations
    E. lack of reasonable precautions

19.____

20. The chemical agent which has been used extensively to prevent the spread of typhus infection is
    A. cortisone
    B. D.D.T.
    C. penicillin
    D. ephedrine
    E. sulfanilamide

20.____

21. The medical term for *hardening of the arteries* is   21.____
    A. carcinoma   B. arthritis   C. thrombosis
    D. arteriosclerosis   E. phlebitis

22. A set of symptoms which occur together is called a   22.____
    A. sympathin   B. syncope   C. syndrome
    D. synecdoche   E. syllogism

23. If the characteristics of a person were being studied by competent observers,   23.____
    it would be expected that their observations would differ MOST markedly with
    respect to their evaluation of the person's
    A. intelligence   B. nutritional characteristics
    C. temperamental characteristics   D. weight
    E. height

24. If there are evidences of dietary deficiency in families where cereals make up   24.____
    a major portion of the diet, the MOST likely reason for this deficiency is that
    A. cereals cause absorption of excessive quantities of water
    B. persons who concentrate their diet on cereals do not chew their food
       properly
    C. carbohydrates are deleterious
    D. other essential food elements are omitted
    E. children eat cereals too rapidly

25. Although malnutrition is generally associated with poverty, dietary studies of   25.____
    population groups in the United States reveal that
    A. malnutrition is most often due to a deficiency of nutrients found chiefly in
       high-cost foods
    B. there has been overemphasis of the causal relationship between poverty
       and malnutrition
    C. malnutrition is found among people with sufficient money to be well fed
    D. a majority of the population in all income groups is undernourished
    E. malnutrition is not a factor in the incidence of rickets

KEY (CORRECT ANSWERS)

1. D
2. B
3. B
4. A
5. D

6. A
7. D
8. E
9. A
10. E

11. B
12. D
13. A
14. D
15. D

16. B
17. C
18. D
19. A
20. B

21. D
22. C
23. C
24. D
25. C

TEST 4

DIRECTIONS: Each question or incomplete statement is followed by several suggested answers or completions. Select the one that BEST answers the question or completes the statement. *PRINT THE LETTER OF THE CORRECT ANSWER IN THE SPACE AT THE RIGHT.*

1. A medically trained person who treats mental diseases is called a(n) 1.____
   - A. psychologist
   - B. sociologist
   - C. psychiatrist
   - D. physiologist
   - E. opthamologist

2. Of the following social agencies, the which must rely MOST on short-contact interviewing is the 2.____
   - A. child-guidance clinic
   - B. Travelers' Aid Society
   - C. Social Service Exchange
   - D. Hospital for Crippled Children
   - E. juvenile court

3. The organization which has as one of its primary functions the mitigation of suffering caused by famine, fire, floods, and other national calamities is the 3.____
   - A. National Safety Council
   - B. Salvation Army
   - C. Public Administration Services
   - D. American National Red Cross
   - E. American Legion

4. The MAIN difference between public welfare and private social agencies is that in public agencies 4.____
   - A. case records are open to the public
   - B. the granting of assistance cannot be sufficiently flexible to meet the varying needs of individual recipients
   - C. only financial assistance may be provided
   - D. all policies and procedures must be based upon statutory authorizations
   - E. economical and efficient administration are stressed because their funds are obtained through public taxation

5. Proper handling of a case in which the applicant requires temporary congregate care would involve a referral initially to 5.____
   - A. a private agency
   - B. a religious institution
   - C. the state welfare agency
   - D. the federal government
   - E. one of the municipal shelters

6. A recipient of relief who is in need of the services on an attorney but is unable to pay the customary fees, should generally be referred to the 6.____
   - A. Small Claims Court
   - B. Domestic Relations Court
   - C. County Lawyers Association
   - D. City Law Department
   - E. Legal Aid Society

7. A person who is not satisfied with the action taken by the Department of Social Services on his application for old-age assistance may appeal to the State Department of Social Welfare for an impartial review and a *fair hearing*. 7.____

The final decision in such a hearing is made by the
- A. State Board of Social Welfare
- B. State Commissioner of Social Welfare
- C. Commissioner of Social Services
- D. Attorney-General of the State
- E. Federal Security Agency

8. An injured worker should file his claim for workmen's compensation with the
   - A. State Labor Relations Board
   - B. Division of Placement and Unemployment Insurance
   - C. State Industrial Commission
   - D. Workmen's Compensation Board
   - E. State Insurance Board

   8._____

9. In order to supplement the care and guidance furnished to young people by the family and other social institutions, the legislature created a temporary agency known as the State Youth Commission.
   Among the powers and duties of this Commission are those listed below, with the EXCEPTION of
   - A. supervising the administration of state institutions for juvenile delinquents
   - B. authorizing payment of state aid to municipalities in accordance with the provisions of the Youth Commission Act
   - C. making studies and recommendations regarding the guidance and treatment of juvenile delinquents
   - D. devising plans for the creation and operation of youth bureaus and recreation projects
   - E. making necessary studies and analyses of the problems of youth guidance and the prevention of juvenile delinquency

   9._____

10. One of the institutions operated by the State Department of Social Welfare is the
    - A. State School for the Blind, Batavia
    - B. State Training School for Boys, Warwick
    - C. State Reconstruction Home, West Haverstraw
    - D. State School for Mental Defectives, Newark
    - E. Woodbourne Institute for Defective Delinquents, Woodbourne

    10._____

11. The one of the following which is NOT included among the responsibilities of the Bureau of Public Assistance of the Social Security Administration is
    - A. reviewing and approving state plans for public assistance and the operation of these plans, in order to determine their continuing conformity to the Social Security Act
    - B. administering provisions for grants by the federal government to states for old-age assistance, aid to the blind, aid to dependent children, and aid to the permanently and totally disabled
    - C. carrying out the Social Security Administration's functions in connection with the federal-state unemployment insurance system

    11._____

D. reviewing state estimates for public assistance and certifying the amount of federal grants to states
E. collecting, analyzing, and publishing data on the operation of all forms of public assistance in the states, including general assistance

12. Because of the number of able-bodied employable persons on relief, the Department of Social Services once adopted the policy of
    A. removing all employables from the relief rolls
    B. subjecting such persons to special review in order to determine whether they are concealing facts about employment
    C. assigning such persons to various city departments for appropriate employment commensurate with the amount of relief grants
    D. forcing all men on the employable list to apply to other governmental agencies as provisional civil service workers
    E. requesting selective service boards to give preference to such employable persons of appropriate age for induction into the armed forces

12.____

13. The type of insurance found MOST frequently among families such as those assisted by the Department of Social Services is
    A. accident
    B. straight life
    C. endowment
    D. industrial
    E. personal liability

13.____

14. Of the following items in the standard budget of the Department of Social Services, the one for which actual expenditures would be MOST constant throughout the year is
    A. fuel
    B. housing
    C. medical care
    D. clothing
    E. household replacements

14.____

15. The MOST frequent cause of *broken homes* is attributed to the
    A. temperamental incompatibilities of parents and in-laws
    B. extension of the system of children's courts
    C. psychopathic irresponsibility of the parents
    D. institutionalization of one of the spouses
    E. death of one or both spouses

15.____

16. In rearing children, the problems of the widower are usually greater than those of the widow, largely because of the
    A. tendency of widowers to impose excessively rigid moral standards
    B. increased economic hardship
    C. added difficulty of maintaining a desirable home
    D. possibility that a stepmother will be added to the household
    E. prevalent masculine prejudice against pursuits which are inherently feminine

16.____

17. Foster-home placement of children is often advocated in preference to institutionalization PRIMARILY because
    A. the law does not provide for local supervision of children's institutions
    B. institutions furnish a more expensive type of care
    C. the number of institutions is insufficient compared to the number of children needing car
    D. children are not well treated in institutions
    E. foster homes provide a more normal environment for children

17.____

18. Of the following, the category MOST likely to yield the greatest reduction in cost to the taxpayer under improved employment conditions is
    A. home relief, including aid to the homeless
    B. aid to the blind
    C. aid to dependent children
    D. old-age assistance
    E. aid to the permanently and totally disabled

18.____

19. One of the MOST common characteristics of the chronic alcoholic is
    A. low intelligence level   B. wanderlust
    C. psychosis   D. independence
    E. egocentricity

19.____

20. Of the following factors leading toward the cure of the alcoholic, the MOST important is thought to be
    A. removal of all alcohol from the immediate environment
    B. development of a sense of personal adequacy
    C. social disapproval of drinking
    D. segregation from former companions
    E. intensive supervision by parole officers

20.____

21. An interview is BEST conducted in private primarily because
    A. the person interviewed will tend to be less self-conscious
    B. the interviewer will be able to maintain his continuity of thought better
    C. it will insure that the interview is *off the record*
    D. people tend to *show off* before an audience
    E. constant interruption by visitors and telephone calls will irritate the interviewer

21.____

22. An interviewer will be better able to understand the person interviewed and his problems if he recognizes that much of the person's behavior is due to motives
    A. which are deliberate   B. of which he is unaware
    C. which are inexplicable   D. which are kept under control
    E. which are calculated to deceive

22.____

23. When an applicant for public assistance is repeatedly told that *everything will be all right*, the effect that can usually be expected is that he will
    A. develop overt negativistic reactions toward the agency
    B. become too closely identified with the interviewer

23.____

C. doubt the interviewer's ability to understand and help with his problems
D. have greater confidence in the interviewer
E. make no appreciable change in his attitude toward the interviewer

24. While interviewing a client, it is preferable that the social service worker
    A. take no notes in order to avoid disturbing the client
    B. focus primary attention on the client while the client is talking
    C. take no notes in order to impress upon the client the worker's ability to remember all the pertinent facts of his case
    D. record all details in order to show the client that what he says is important
    E. record all details in order to impress upon the client the official character of his statements

25. During an interview, a curious applicant asks several questions about the social service worker's private life.
    As the interviewer, you should
    A. refuse to answer such questions
    B. answer his questions fully
    C. explain that your primary concern is with his problems and that discussion of your personal affairs will not be helpful in meeting his needs
    D. explain that it is the responsibility of the interviewer to ask questions and not to answer them
    E. answer only enough of his questions to the extent necessary to establish a friendly relationship with him

KEY (CORRECT ANSWERS)

1.	C	11.	C
2.	B	12.	C
3.	D	13.	D
4.	D	14.	B
5.	E	15.	E
6.	E	16.	C
7.	B	17.	E
8.	D	18.	A
9.	A	19.	E
10.	B	20.	B

21. A
22. B
23. C
24. C
25. C

TEST 5

DIRECTIONS: Each question or incomplete statement is followed by several suggested answers or completions. Select the one that BEST answers the question or completes the statement. *PRINT THE LETTER OF THE CORRECT ANSWER IN THE SPACE AT THE RIGHT.*

1. An interviewer can BEST establish a good relationship with the person being interviewed by
   A. assuming casual interest in the statements made by the person being interviewed
   B. asking questions which enable the person to show pride in his knowledge
   C. taking the point of view of the person interviewed
   D. controlling the interview to a major extent
   E. showing a genuine interest in the person

   1.____

2. An interviewer's attention must be directed toward himself as well as toward the person interviewed.
   This statement means that the interviewer should
   A. keep in mind the extent to which his own prejudices may influence his judgment
   B. rationalize the statements made by the person interviewed
   C. gain the respect and confidence of the person interviewed
   D. avoid being too impersonal
   E. avoid using indirect methods in eliciting information from the person interviewed

   2.____

3. More complete expression will be obtained from a person being interviewed if the interviewer can create the impression that
   A. the data secured will become part of a permanent record
   B. official information must be accurate in every detail
   C. it is the duty of the person interviewed to give accurate data
   D. the interviewer checks additional sources to get complete data
   E. the person interviewed is participating in a discussion of his own problems

   3.____

4. The practice of asking leading questions should be avoided in an interview because the
   A. interviewer risks revealing his attitudes to the person being interviewed
   B. interviewer may be led to ignore the objective attitudes of the person interviewed
   C. answers may be unwarrantedly influenced
   D. person interviewed will resent the attempt to lead him and will be less cooperative
   E. replies to such questions are always verbose

   4.____

5. A good technique for the interviewer to use in an effort to secure reliable data and to reduce the possibility of misunderstanding is to
   A. use casual undirected conversation, enabling the person being interviewed to talk about himself, and thus secure the desired information
   B. adopt the procedure of using direct questions regularly
   C. extract the desired information from the person being interviewed by putting him on the defensive
   D. explain to the person being interviewed the information desired and the reason for needing it
   E. explain that he is an experienced interviewer and can detect false statements

5.____

6. As a social service worker interviewing an applicant for public assistance, your attitude toward his veracity should be that the information he has furnished you is
   A. *untruthful* until you have had an opportunity to check the information
   B. *truthful* only insofar as verifiable facts are concerned
   C. *untruthful* because clients tend to interpret everything in their own favor
   D. *truthful* until you have information to the contrary
   E. *untruthful* because most applicants are unreliable

6.____

7. When a public assistance agency assigns its most experienced interviewers to conduct initial interviews with applicants, the MOST important reason for its action is that
   A. experienced workers are always older, and therefore command the respect of applicants
   B. the applicant may be given a complete understanding of the procedures to be followed and the time involved in obtaining assistance payments
   C. applicants with fraudulent intentions will be detected, and prevented from obtaining further services from the agency
   D. the agency may immediately obtain an accurate and complete plan to be followed in giving assistance to the applicant
   E. the applicant may be given an understanding of the purpose of the assistance program and of the bases for granting assistance, in addition to the routine information

7.____

8. As a social service worker conducting the first interview with an applicant for public assistance, you should
   A. ask questions requiring *yes* or *no* answers in order to simplify the interview
   B. rephrase several of the key questions as a check on his previous statements
   C. let him tell his own story while keeping him to the relevant facts
   D. avoid showing any sympathy for the applicant while he is revealing his personal needs and problems
   E. ask only direct questions so as to demonstrate your impersonal approach

8.____

9. An aged person who is unable to produce immediate proof of age has made an application for old-age assistance. He states that it will take about a week to obtain the necessary proof and that he does not have enough money to provide meals for himself until then.
If it appears that he is in immediate need, he should be told that
   A. the law requires proof of age before any assistance can be granted
   B. temporary assistance will be provided pending the completion of the investigation
   C. a personal loan will be provided from a revolving fund
   D. he should arrange for a small loan from private sources
   E. he will have to produce an affidavit witnessed by two relatives who will vouch for the accuracy of his statements before any assistance can be provided

10. If the social service worker learns during the interview that the client has applied for public assistance without the knowledge of her husband, even though he is a member of the same household, the worker should
   A. appear not to notice this oversight, but watch for other evidences of marital discord
   B. make no mention of this to the applicant, but before taking final action send a note to the husband asking him to come in
   C. discuss this situation with the client and help her recognize the value of her husband's participation in the application
   D. point out to the applicant the implications of her behavior and ask for an explanation of her motives
   E. tell the applicant that the husband's needs will be excluded from the budget until he appears for a personal interview

11. Responsibility for fully informing the public about the availability of public assistance can MOST successfully be discharged by
   A. local public assistance agencies   B. social service exchanges
   C. community chest organizations   D. councils of social agencies
   E. service clubs

12. Of the sources through which a welfare agency can seek information about the family background and economic needs of a particular client, the MOST important consists of
   A. records and documents covering the client
   B. interviews with the client's relatives
   C. the client's own story
   D. direct contacts with former employers
   E. information offered by the client's neighbors

13. The one of the following sources of evidence which would MOST likely to give information needed to verify residence is
   A. family affidavits   B. medical and hospital bills
   C. an original birth certificate D. rental receipts
   E. an insurance policy

14. In public assistance agencies, vital statistics are a resource used by the workers MAINLY to
    A. help establish eligibility through verification of births, deaths, and marriages
    B. help establish eligibility through verification of divorce proceedings
    C. secure proof of unemployment and eligibility for unemployment compensation
    D. secure indices of the cost of living in the larger cities
    E. discourage applications from ineligible persons

15. Case record should be considered confidential in order to
    A. make it impossible for agencies to know each other's methods
    B. permit worker to make objective rather than subjective comments
    C. prevent recipients from comparing amounts of assistance given to different families
    D. keep pertinent information from other social workers
    E. protect clients and their families

16. Because the social service worker generally is not trained as a psychiatrist, he should, when encountering psychiatric problems in the performance of his departmental duties,
    A. ignore such problems because they are beyond the scope of his responsibilities
    B. inform the affected persons that he recognizes their problems personally but will take no official cognizance of them
    C. ask to be relieved of the cases in which these problems are met and recommend that they be assigned to a psychiatrist
    D. recognize such problems where they exist and make referrals to the proper sources for treatment
    E. ask his supervisor to assign a psychiatric case worker to accompany him on all subsequent visits to the client

17. The family budget is a device used by the Department of Social Services to
    A. determine changes in the cost-of-living index
    B. estimate the needs of families and the amount of assistance necessary to meet this needs
    C. evaluate its financial condition
    D. estimate probable expenditures during a given period
    E. determine whether an applicant is eligible for categorical assistance or for general relief

18. The amount included for food for each client in Department of Social Services budgets should
    A. be based on quantitative caloric estimates of energy requirements rather than on variety in the kinds of foods
    B. be high enough to provide minimum subsistence, but low enough to discourage ineligible applicants
    C. exclude special dietary needs which are relatively expensive

D. cover food idiosyncrasies of various members of the household
E. meet the generally accepted standards for proper nutrition

19. The program for aid to dependent children is PRIMARILY directed toward
    A. the placement and supervision of children in selected foster homes
    B. provision of assistance whereby children can remain in their own homes or in the homes of relatives
    C. rehabilitation of neglected and delinquent children
    D. provision of specialized services to children in areas of special need
    E. provision of assistance to widows of good moral character for the care of their children

19.____

20. Since need is a condition of eligibility in the old-age assistance program, an assistance payment to an aged recipient should be based upon a consideration of
    A. the length of time he received general relief prior to his application for old-age assistance
    B. his attitude toward the agency
    C. his total needs and resources
    D. the probable duration of his dependency
    E. the average monthly cost of institutional care

20.____

21. From a social point of view, the reason for the growth of the practice of giving public assistance in the form of cash payments is the
    A. resultant reduction in complaints coming to the agency
    B. increased necessity for developing nationwide comparative statistics
    C. facilitation of recovery for relief improperly granted
    D. public's increasing belief in the essential justice of this type of assistance

21.____

22. In closing the case of a client, the social service worker should attempt to give the client a(n)
    A. feeling of being rejected by the agency as a worthy person
    B. idea of the progress of similar cases being handled by the agency
    C. understanding that his case could be reopened for full relief, if necessary, but not for emergency assistance
    D. explanation of the conditions upon which he might make re-application
    E. explanation of the limitations of the agency in meeting his needs

22.____

23. There is widespread agreement among nearly all planning groups concerned with public assistance that
    A. need for public assistance should be the primary, if not the only, condition of eligibility; and that all arbitrary conditions of eligibility such as citizenship, ownership of home, and moral character should be eliminated from all public assistance programs
    B. public assistance grants should be paid by voucher rather than in cash because most recipients do not use cash allowances for the purposes for which they are intended
    C. the names of persons receiving public assistance should be publicized in order to prevent fraud

23.____

D. public assistance should be discontinued immediately whenever the unemployed father of a family receiving assistance refuses a job offer
E. public assistance should not be provided for any persons who own property or who have any financial resources

24. Of fundamental importance to the work of social worker in the Department of Social Services is
    A. the knowledge of when to use the power of the Department to subdue an angry client
    B. an ability to classify clients according to common characteristics as described in case records
    C. the ability to explain eligibility in terms of legal requirements with clarity and simplicity
    D. the realization that persons who apply for public assistance have become independent because of lack of industriousness and are therefore unable to manage their own affairs
    E. a general knowledge of the executive, administrative, and supervisory functions of the Department

24.____

25. Although a social worker in the Department of Social Services has several responsibilities, his PRIMARY one is to
    A. nullify any restrictive rules and regulations issued by the State Department of Social Welfare
    B. carry out his own interpretation of the function of the Department of Social Services
    C. carry out the objectives of Department of Social Services programs as set forth in the Social Welfare Law
    D. avoid community criticism of the manner in which the programs of the Department of Social Services are conducted
    E. give relief to all applicants who claim they are eligible

25.____

KEY (CORRECT ANSWERS)

1.	E		11.	A
2.	A		12.	C
3.	E		13.	D
4.	C		14.	A
5.	D		15.	E
6.	D		16.	D
7.	E		17.	B
8.	C		18.	E
9.	B		19.	B
10.	C		20.	C

21. D
22. D
23. A
24. C
25. C

EXAMINATION SECTION
TEST 1

DIRECTIONS: Each question or incomplete statement is followed by several suggested answers or completions. Select the one that BEST answers the question or completes the statement. *PRINT THE LETTER OF THE CORRECT ANSWER IN THE SPACE AT THE RIGHT.*

1. When a worker is planning a future interview with a client, of the following, the MOST important consideration is the
    A. recommendations he will make to the client
    B. place where the client will be interviewed
    C. purpose for which the client will be interviewed
    D. personality of the client

    1.____

2. For a worker to make a practice of reviewing the client's case record, if available, prior to the interview is usually
    A. *inadvisable*, because knowledge of the client's past record will tend to influence the worker's judgment
    B. *advisable*, because knowledge of the client's background will help the worker to identify discrepancies in the client's responses
    C. *inadvisable*, because such review is time-consuming and of questionable value
    D. *advisable*, because knowledge of the client's background will help the worker to understand the client's situation

    2.____

3. Assume that a worker makes a practice of constantly re-assuring clients with serious and complex problems by making such statements as: *I'm sure you'll soon be well; I know you'll get a job soon*; or *Everything will be all right*.
    Of the following, the MOST likely result of such practice is to
    A. encourage the client and make him feel that the worker understands what the client is going through
    B. make the client doubtful about the worker's understanding of his difficulties and the worker's ability to help
    C. confuse the client and cause him to hesitate to take any action on his own initiative
    D. help the client to be more realistic about his situation and the probability that it will improve

    3.____

4. In order to get the maximum amount of information from a client during an interview, of the following, it is MOST important for the worker to communicate to the client the feeling that the worker is
    A. interested in the client
    B. a figure of authority
    C. efficient in his work habits
    D. sympathetic to the client's lifestyle

    4.____

5. Of the following, the worker who takes extremely detailed notes during an interview with a client is MOST likely to
   A. encourage the client to talk freely
   B. distract and antagonize the client
   C. help the client feel at ease
   D. understand the client's feelings

6. You find that many of the clients you interview are verbally abusive and unusually hostile to you.
   Of the following, the MOST appropriate action for you to take FIRST is to
   A. review your interviewing techniques and consider whether you may be provoking these clients
   B. act in a more authoritative manner when interviewing troublesome clients
   C. tell these clients that you will not process their applications unless their troublesome behavior ceases
   D. disregard the clients' troublesome behavior during the interviews

7. During an interview, you did not completely understand several of your client's responses. In each instance, you rephrased the client's statement and asked the client if that was what he meant.
   For you to use such a technique during interviews would be considered
   A. *inappropriate*; you may have distorted the client's meaning by rephrasing his statements
   B. *inappropriate*; you should have asked the same question until you received a comprehensible response
   C. *appropriate*; the client will have a chance to correct you if you have misinterpreted his responses
   D. *appropriate*; a worker should rephrase clients' responses for the records

8. A worker is interviewing a client who has just had a severe emotional shock because of an assault on her by a mugger.
   Of the following, the approach which would generally be MOST helpful to the client is for the worker to
   A. comfort the client and encourage her to talk about the assault
   B. sympathize with the client but refuse to talk about the assault
   C. tell the client to control her emotions and think positively about the future
   D. proceed with the interview in an impersonal and unemotional manner

9. A worker finds that her questions are misinterpreted by many of the clients she interviews.
   Of the following, the MOST likely reason for this problem is that the
   A. client is not listening attentively
   B. client wants to avoid the subject being discussed
   C. worker has failed to express her meaning clearly
   D. worker has failed to put the client at ease

3 (#1)

10. For a worker to look directly at the client and observe him during the interview is, generally,
    A. *inadvisable*; this will make the client nervous and uncomfortable
    B. *advisable*; the client will be more likely to refrain from lying
    C. *inadvisable*; the worker will not be able to take notes for the case record
    D. *advisable*; this will encourage conversation and accelerate the progress of the interview

10.____

11. You are interviewing a client who is applying for social services for the first time. In order to encourage this client to freely give you the information needed for you to establish his eligibility, of the following, the BEST way to start the interview is by
    A. asking questions the client can easily answer
    B. conveying the impression that his responses to your questions will be checked
    C. asking two or three similar but important questions
    D. assuring the client that your sole responsibility is *getting the facts*

11.____

12. Workers are encouraged to record significant information obtained from clients and services provided for clients.
    Of the following, the MOST important reason for this practice is that these case records will
    A. help to reduce the need for regular supervisory conferences
    B. indicate to workers which clients are taking up the most time
    C. provide information which will help the agency to improve its services to clients
    D. make it easier to verify the complaints of clients

12.____

13. As a worker in the employment eligibility section, you find that interviews can be completed in a shorter period of time if you ask questions which limit the client to a certain answer.
    For you to use such a technique would be considered
    A. *inappropriate*, because this type of question usually requires advance preparation
    B. *inappropriate*, because this type of question may inhibit the client from saying what he really means
    C. *appropriate*, because you know the areas into which the questions should be directed
    D. *appropriate*, because this type of question usually helps clients to express themselves clearly

13.____

14. Assume that a worker at a juvenile detention center is planning foster care placement for a child.
    For the worker to have the child participate in the planning is generally considered to be
    A. time-consuming and of little practical value in preparing the child for placement
    B. valuable in helping the child adjust to future placement

14.____

C. useful, because the child will be more likely to cooperate with others in the center
D. anxiety-provoking because the child will feel that he has been abandoned

15. You have been assigned to interview the mother of a five-year-old son in her home to get information useful in locating the child's absent father. During the interview, you notice many serious bruises on the child's arms and legs, which the mother explains are due to the child's clumsiness.
Of the following, your BEST course of action is to
    A. accept the mother's explanation and concentrate on getting information which will help you to locate the father
    B. advise the mother to have the child examined for a medical condition that may be causing his clumsiness
    C. make a surprise visit to the mother later, to see whether someone is beating the child
    D. complete your interview with the mother and report the case to your supervisor for investigation of possible child abuse

16. During an interview, the former landlord of an absent father offers to help you to locate the father if you will give the landlord confidential information you have on the financial situation of the father.
Of the following, you should
    A. immediately end the interview with the landlord
    B. urge the landlord to help you but explain that you are not permitted to give him confidential information
    C. freely give the landlord the confidential information he requests about the father
    D. give the landlord the information only if he promises to keep it confidential

17. You feel that your client, a released mental patient, is not adjusting well to living on his own in an apartment. To gather more information, you interview privately his next-door neighbor, who claims that the client is creating a disturbance and speaks of the client in an angry and insulting manner.
Of the following, the BEST action for you to take in this situation is to
    A. listen patiently to the neighbor to try to get the facts about your client's behavior
    B. inform the neighbor that he has no right to speak insultingly about a mentally ill person
    C. make an appointment to interview the neighbor some other time when he isn't so upset
    D. tell the neighbor that you were not aware of the client's behavior and that you will have the client moved

18. As a worker assigned to an income maintenance center, you are interviewing a client to determine his eligibility for a work program. Suddenly, the client begins to shout that he is in no condition to work and that you are persecuting him for no reason.

Of the following, your BEST response to this client is to
- A. advise the client to stop shouting or you will call for the security guard
- B. wait until the client calms down, then order him to come back for another interview
- C. insist that you are not persecuting the client and that he must complete the interview
- D. wait until the client calms down, say that you understand how he feels, and try to continue the interview

19. You are counseling a mother whose 17-year-old son has recently been returned home from a mental institution. Although she is willing to care for her son at home, she is frightened by his strange and sometimes violent behavior and does not know the best arrangement to make for his care.
Of the following, your MOST appropriate response to this mother's problem is to
    - A. describe the supportive services and alternatives to home care which are available
    - B. help her to accept her son's strange and violent behavior
    - C. tell her that she will not be permitted to care for her son at home if she is frightened by his behavior
    - D. convince her that she is not responsible for her son's mental condition

20. Assume that, as an intake worker, you are interviewing an elderly man who comes to the center several times a month to discuss topics with you which are not related to social service. You realize that the man is lonely and enjoys these conversations.
Of the following, it would be MOST appropriate to
    - A. politely discourage the man from coming in to pass the time with you
    - B. avoid speaking to this man the next time he comes into the center
    - C. explore with the client his feelings about joining a Senior Citizens' Center
    - D. continue to hold these conversations with the man

21. A client you are interviewing in the housing elibility section tends to ramble on after each response that he gives, so that man clients are kept waiting.
In this situation, of the following, it would be MOST advisable to
    - A. try to direct the interview, in order to obtain the necessary information
    - B. reduce the number of questions asked so that you can shorten the interview
    - C. arrange a second interview for the client so that you can give him more time
    - D. tell the client that he is wasting everybody's time

22. A non-minority worker in an employment eligibility unit is about to interview a minority client on public assistance for job placement when the client says:
What does your kind know about my problems? You've never had to survive out on these streets.
Of the following, the worker's MOST appropriate response to this situation is to

A. postpone the interview until a minority worker is available to interview the client
B. tell the client that he must cooperate with the worker if he wants to continue receiving public assistance
C. explain to the client the function of the worker in this unit and the services he provides
D. assure the client that you do not have to be a member of a minority group to understand the effects of poverty

23. As a worker in a family services unit, you have been assigned to follow-up a case folder recently forwarded from the protective-diagnostic unit.
After making appropriate clerical notations in your records such as name of client and date of receipt, which of the following would be the MOST appropriate step to take next?
    A. Confer with your supervisor
    B. Read and review all reports included in the case folder
    C. Arrange to visit with the client at his home
    D. Confer with representatives of any other agencies which have been in contact with the client

24. As a worker in the employment section, you are interviewing a young client who seriously underestimates the amount of education and training he will require for a certain occupation.
For you to tell the client that you think he is mistaken would, generally, be considered
    A. *inadvisable*, because workers should not express their opinions to clients
    B. *inadvisable*, because clients have the right to self-determination
    C. *advisable*, because clients should generally be alerted to their misconceptions
    D. *advisable*, because workers should convince clients to adopt a proper lifestyle

25. As an intake worker, you are counseling a mother and her unmarried, thirteen-year-old daughter, who is six months pregnant, concerning the advisability of placing the daughter's baby for adoption. The mother insists on adoption, but the daughter remains silent and appears undecided.
Of the following, you should encourage the daughter to
    A. make the final decision on adoption herself
    B. keep her baby despite her mother's insistence on adoption
    C. accept her mother's insistence on adoption
    D. make the decision on adoption together with her mother

KEY (CORRECT ANSWERS)

1.	C		11.	A
2.	D		12.	C
3.	B		13.	B
4.	A		14.	B
5.	B		15.	D
6.	A		16.	B
7.	C		17.	A
8.	A		18.	D
9.	C		19.	A
10.	D		20.	C

21. A
22. C
23. B
24. C
25. D

TEST 2

DIRECTIONS: Each question or incomplete statement is followed by several suggested answers or completions. Select the one that BEST answers the question or completes the statement. *PRINT THE LETTER OF THE CORRECT ANSWER IN THE SPACE AT THE RIGHT.*

1. You are interviewing a legally responsible absent father who refuses to make child support payments because he claims the mother physically abuses the child.
   Of the following, the BEST way for you to handle his situation is to tell the father that you
   A. will report his complaint about the mother, but he is still responsible for making child support payments
   B. suspect that he is complaining about the mother in order to avoid his own responsibility for making child support payments
   C. are concerned with his responsibility to make child support payments, not with the mother's abuse of the child
   D. cannot determine his responsibility for making child support payments until his complaint about the mother is investigated

   1.____

2. On a visit to a home where child abuse is alleged, you find the mother preparing lunch for her two children. She tells you that she knows that a neighbor is spreading lies about her treatment of the children.
   Which one of the following is the BEST action for you to take?
   A. Thank the mother for her assistance, leave the home, and indicate in your report that the allegation of child abuse is false
   B. Tell the mother that, since you have been sent to visit her, there must be some truth to the allegations
   C. Explain the purpose of your visit and observe whatever interaction takes place between the children and the mother
   D. Conclude the interview, since you have observed the mother preparing a good lunch for the children

   2.____

3. You are interviewing an elderly woman who lives alone to determine her eligibility for homemaker service at public expense. Though obviously frail and in need of this service, the woman is not completely cooperative, and, during the interview, is often silent for a considerable period of time.
   Of the following, the BEST way for you to deal with these periods of silence is to
   A. realize that she may be embarrassed to have to apply for homemaker service at public expense, and emphasize her right to this service
   B. postpone the interview and make an appointment with her for a later date, when she may be better able to cooperate
   C. explain to the woman that you have many clients to interview and need her cooperation to complete the interview quickly
   D. recognize that she is probably hiding something and begin to ask questions to draw her out

   3.____

4. During a conference with an adolescent boy at a juvenile detention center, you find out for the first time that he would prefer to be placed in foster care rather than return to his natural parents.
To uncover the reasons why the boy dislikes his own home, of the following, it would be MOST advisable for you to
   A. ask the boy a number of short, simple questions about his feelings
   B. encourage the boy to talk freely and express his feelings as best he can
   C. interview the parents and find out why the boy doesn't want to live at home
   D. administer a battery of psychological tests in order to make an assessment of the boy's problems

5. Of the following, the BEST way to determine which activities should be provided for members of a Senior Citizens' Center is to
   A. ask the neighborhood community board to submit their recommendations
   B. meet with the professional staff of the center to get their opinions
   C. encourage the members of the center to express their personal preferences
   D. study the schedules prepared by other Senior Citizens' Centers for guidance

6. You are interviewing a mother who is applying for Aid to Families with Dependent Children because the husband has deserted the family. The mother becomes annoyed at having to answer your questions and tells you to leave her apartment.
Which one of the following actions would be MOST appropriate to take FIRST in this situation?
   A. Return to the office and close the case for lack of cooperation
   B. Tell the mother that you will get the information from her neighbors if she does not cooperate
   C. Tell the mother that you must stay until you get answers to your questions
   D. Explain to the mother the reasons for the interview and the consequences of her failure to cooperate

7. A worker assigned to visit homebound clients to determine their eligibility for Medicaid must understand each client's situation as completely as possible.
Of the following source which may provide insight into the client's situation, the one that is generally MOST revealing is:
   A. Close relatives of the client, who have known him for many years
   B. Next-door neighbors, who have observed the daily living habits of the client
   C. The client himself, who can provide his own description of his situation
   D. The records of other social agencies that may have served the client

8. A worker counseling juvenile clients finds that, although he can tolerate most of their behavior, he becomes infuriated when they lie to him.
Of the following, the worker can BEST deal with his anger at his clients' lying by

A. recognizing his feelings of anger and learning to control expression of these feelings to his clients
B. warning his clients that he cannot be responsible for his anger when a client lies to him
C. using willpower to suppress his feelings of anger when a client lies to him
D. realizing that lying is a common trait of juveniles and not directed against him personally

9. During an interview at the employment eligibility section, one of your clients, a former drug addict, has expressed an interest in attending a community counseling center and resuming his education.
In this case, the MOST appropriate action that you should take FIRST is to
   A. determine whether this ambition is realistic for a former drug addict
   B. send the client's application to a community counseling center which provides services to former addicts
   C. ask the client whether he is really motivated or is just seeking your approval
   D. encourage and assist the client to take this step, since his interest is a positive sign

10. Because of habitual neglect by his mother, a five-year-old boy has been placed in a foster home.
For the worker to encourage the mother to visit the boy in the foster home is, generally,
   A. *desirable*, because the boy will be helped by continuing his ties with his mother
   B. *undesirable*, because the boy will be upset by his mother's visits and will have a harder time adjusting to the foster home
   C. *desirable*, because the mother will learn from the foster parents how she should treat the boy
   D. *undesirable*, because the mother should be punished for her neglect of the boy by complete separation from him

11. You are interviewing a client who, during previous appointments, has not responded to your requests for information required to determine his continued eligibility for services. On this occasion, the client again offers an excuse which you feel is not acceptable.
For you to advise the client of the probable loss of services because of his lack of cooperation is
   A. *inappropriate*, because the threat to withhold services will harm the relationship between worker and client
   B. *inappropriate*, because workers should not reveal to clients that they do not believe their statements
   C. *appropriate*, because social services are a reward given to cooperative clients
   D. *appropriate*, because the worker should inform clients of the consequences of their lack of cooperation

4 (#2)

12. Assume that you are counseling an adolescent boy in a juvenile detention center who has been a ringleader in smuggling pot into the center.
During your regular interview with this boy, of the following, it would be *advisable* to
    A. tell him you know that he has been involved in smuggling pot and that you are trying to understand the reasons for his misbehavior
    B. ignore his pot smuggling in order to reassure him that you understand and accept him, even though you do not agree with his standards of behavior
    C. warn him that you have reported his pot smuggling and that he will be punished for his misbehavior
    D. show him that you disagree of his pot smuggling, but assure him that you will not report him for his misbehavior

13. Your unit has received several complaints about a homeless elderly woman living outdoors in various locations in the area. To help determine the need for protective services for this woman, you interview several persons in the neighborhood who are familiar with her, but all are uncooperative or reluctant to give information.
Of the following, your BEST approach to these persons is to explain to them that
    A. you will take legal steps against them if they do not cooperate with you
    B. their cooperation may enable you to help this homeless woman
    C. you need their cooperation to remove this homeless woman from their neighborhood
    D. they will be responsible for any harm that comes to this homeless woman

14. A foster mother complains to the worker that a ten-year-old boy placed with her is overaggressive and unmanageable. The worker, knowing that the boy has been placed unsuccessfully several times before, constantly reassures the foster mother that the boy is improving steadily.
For the worker to do this, generally,
    A. *good practice*, because the foster mother may accept the professional opinion of the worker and keep the boy
    B. *poor practice*, because the foster mother may be discouraged from discussing the boy's problems with the worker
    C. *good practice*, because the foster mother may feel guilty if she gives up the boy when he is improving
    D. *poor practice*, because the boy should not remain with a foster mother who complains about his behavior

15. Assume that, as a worker in the liaison and adjustment unit, you are interviewing a client regarding an adjustment in budget. The client begins to scream at you that she holds you responsible for the decrease in her allowance.
Of the following, which is the BEST way for you to handle this situation?
    A. Attempt to discuss the matter calmly with the client and explain her right to a hearing
    B. Urge the client to appeal and assure her of your support

C. Tell the client that her disorderly behavior will be held against her
D. Tell the client that the reduction is due to red tape and is not your fault

16. As a worker assigned to a juvenile detention center, you are having a counseling interview with a recently admitted boy who is having serious problems in adjusting to confinement in the center. During the interview, the boy frequently interrupts to ask you personal questions.
Of the following, the BEST way for you to deal with these questions is to
   A. tell him in a friendly way that your job is to discuss his problems, not yours
   B. try to understand how the questions relate to the boy's own problems and reply with discretion
   C. take no notice of the questions and continue with the interview
   D. try to win the boy's confidence by answering his questions in detail

16.____

17. A worker is interviewing an elderly woman who hesitates to provide necessary information about her finances to determine whether she is eligible for supplementary assistance. She fears that this information will be reported to others and that her neighbors will find out that she is destitute and applying for welfare.
Of the following, the worker's MOST appropriate response is to
   A. tell her that, if she hesitates to give this information, the agency will get it from other sources
   B. assure her that this information is kept strictly confidential, and will not be given to unauthorized persons
   C. convince her that her application will be turned down unless she provides this information as soon as possible
   D. ask for the name and address of her nearest relative and obtain the information from that person

17.____

18. You are counseling a couple whose children have been placed in a foster home because of the couple's quarrelling and child neglect. When you interview the wife by herself, she tells you that she knows the husband often cheats on her with other women, but she is too afraid of the husband's temper to tell him how much this hurts her.
For you to immediately reveal to the husband the wife's unhappiness concerning his cheating is, generally,
   A. *good practice*, because it will help the husband to understand why his wife quarrels with him
   B. *poor practice*, because information received from the wife should not be given to the husband without her permission
   C. *good practice*, because the husband will direct his anger at you rather than at his wife
   D. *poor practice*, because the wife may have told you a false story about her husband in order to win your sympathy

18.____

6 (#2)

19. A worker in an employment eligibility section is beginning a job placement interview with a tall, strongly-built young man. As the man sits down, the worker comments: *I know a big fellow like you wouldn't be interested in any clerical job.*
For the worker to make such a comment is, generally,
   A. *appropriate*, because it creates an air of familiarity which may put the man at ease
   B. *inappropriate*, because the man may be sensitive about his physical size
   C. *appropriate*, because the worker is using his judgment to help speed up the interview
   D. *inappropriate*, because the man may feel he is being pressured into agreeing with the worker

19.____

20. Workers at a juvenile detention center are responsible for establishing constructive relationships with the youths confined to the center in order to help them adjust to detention.
Of the following, the BEST way for a worker to deal with a youth who acts over-aggressive and hostile is to
   A. take appropriate disciplinary measures
   B. attempt to distract the youth by encouraging him to engage in physical sports
   C. try to discover the real reasons for the youth's hostile behavior
   D. urge the youth to express his anger against the institution instead of *taking it out* on you

20.____

21. A worker in a men's shelter is counseling a middle-aged client for alcoholism. During counseling, the client confesses that, many years ago, he had often enjoyed sexually abusing his ten-year-old daughter. The worker tells the client that he personally finds the client's behavior *morally disgusting*.
For the worker to tell the client this is, generally,
   A. *acceptable counseling practice*, because it may encourage the client to feel guilty about his behavior
   B. *unacceptable counseling practice*, because the client may try to shock the worker by confessing other similar behavior
   C. *acceptable counseling practice*, because *letting off steam* in this manner may relieve tension between the worker and the client
   D. *unacceptable counseling practice*, because the client may hesitate to discuss his behavior frankly with the worker in the future

21.____

22. During your discussion with a foster mother who has had a nine-year-old boy in placement for about one month, you are told that the child is disruptive in school and has been unruly and hostile toward the foster family. The boy had been quiet and docile before placement.
In this situation, it would be MOST appropriate to suggest to the foster mother that
   A. this behavior is normal for a nine-year-old boy
   B. children placed in foster homes usually go through a period of testing their foster parents

22.____

C. the child must have picked up these patterns from the foster family
D. this behavior is probably a sign that she is too strict with the boy

23. During an interview in the housing eligibility section, your client, who wants to move to a larger apartment, asks you to decide on a suitable neighborhood for her.
   For you, the worker, to make such a decision for the client would generally be considered
   A. *appropriate*, because you can save time and expense by sharing your knowledge of neighborhoods with the client
   B. *inappropriate*, because workers should not help clients with this type of decision
   C. *appropriate*, because this will help the client to develop confidence in her ability to make decisions
   D. *inappropriate*, because the client should be encouraged to accept the responsibility of making this decision

24. Your client, an elderly man left unable to care for himself after a stroke, has been referred for home-attendant services, but insists that he does not need these services. You believe that the man considers this to be an insult to his pride and that he will not allow himself to admit that he needs help.
   Of the following, the MOST appropriate action for you to take is to
   A. withdraw the referral for home-attendant services and allow the client to try to take care of himself
   B. process the request for home-attendant services on the assumption that the client will soon realize that he cannot care for himself
   C. discuss with the client your interpretation of his problem and attempt to persuade him to accept home-attendant services
   D. tell the client that he will have no further opportunity to apply for home-attendant services if he does not accept them at this time

25. A worker making a field visit to investigate a complaint of child abuse finds that the parents of the child are a racially mixed couple. The child appears poorly dressed and unruly.
   Of the following, the MOST appropriate approach for the worker to take in this situation is to
   A. take the child aside and ask him privately if either of his parents ever mistreats him
   B. determine if prejudice against the couple has led them to use the child as a scapegoat
   C. question the non-minority parent closely for signs of resentment of the child's mixed parentage
   D. observe the relationship between parents and child for indications of abuse by the parents

KEY (CORRECT ANSWERS)

1.	A		11.	D
2.	C		12.	A
3.	A		13.	B
4.	B		14.	B
5.	C		15.	A
6.	D		16.	B
7.	C		17.	B
8.	A		18.	B
9.	D		19.	D
10.	A		20.	C

21. D
22. B
23. D
24. C
25. D

EXAMINATION SECTION
TEST 1

DIRECTIONS: Each question or incomplete statement is followed by several suggested answers or completions. Select the one that BEST answers the question or completes the statement. *PRINT THE LETTER OF THE CORRECT ANSWER IN THE SPACE AT THE RIGHT.*

1. The basic principle underlying a social security program is that the government should provide
   A. aid to families that is not dependent on state or local participation
   B. assistance to any worthy family unable to maintain itself independently
   C. protection to individuals against some of the social risks that are inherent in an industrialized society
   D. safeguards against those factors leading to economic depression

   1.____

2. The activities of state and local public welfare agencies are dependent to a large degree on the public assistance program of the federal government. The one of the following which the federal government has NOT been successful in achieving within the local agencies is the
   A. broadening of the scope of public assistance administration
   B. expansion of the categorical programs
   C. improvement of the quality of service given to clients
   D. standardization of the administration of general assistance programs

   2.____

3. Of the following statements, the one which BEST describes the federal government's position, as stated in the Social Security Act with regard to tests of character or fitness to be administered by local or state welfare departments to prospective clients is that
   A. no tests of character are required, but they are not specifically prohibited
   B. if tests of character are used, they must be uniform throughout the state
   C. tests of character are contrary to the philosophy of the federal government and are to be considered illegal
   D. no tests of character are required, and assistance to those states that use them will be withheld

   3.____

4. The two factors which are MOST likely to determine the size and cost of a public assistance program are the
   A. size of the staff and its degree of professionalization
   B. form of the grant and the method of disbursement
   C. number of clients accepted and their previous standard of living
   D. conditions of eligibility and the standard of living deemed proper for relief recipients

   4.____

5. One of the criticisms leveled against the program of Medical Assistance for the Aged is that it
   A. receives more federal and state reimbursement than the Old Age Assistance program
   B. does not include persons who formerly received hospital care at total city expense
   C. is unnecessarily restrictive and requires a full welfare scrutiny of the resources of the applicant and his relatives

5.____

6. An increase in the size of the welfare grant may increase the cost of the welfare program not only in terms of those already on the welfare rolls, but because it may result in an increase in the number of people on the rolls.
   The CHIEF reason that an increase in the size of the grant may cause an increase in the number of people on the rolls is that the increased grant may
   A. induce low-salaried wage earners to apply for assistance rather than continue at their menial jobs
   B. make eligible for assistance many people whose resources are just above the previous standard
   C. induce many people to apply for assistance who hesitated to do so because of meagerness of the previous grant
   D. make relatives less willing to contribute because the welfare grant can more adequately cover their dependent's need

6.____

7. One of the MAIN differences between the use of casework methods by a public welfare agency and by a private welfare agency is that the public welfare agency
   A. requires that the applicant be eligible for the services it offers
   B. cannot maintain a non-judgmental attitude toward its clients because of legal requirements
   C. places less emphasis on efforts to change the behavior of its clients
   D. must be more objective in its approach to the client because public funds are involved

7.____

8. All definitions of social casework include certain major assumptions.
   Of the following, the one which is NOT considered a major assumption is that
   A. the individual and society are interdependent
   B. social forces influence behavior and attitudes, affording opportunity for self-development and contribution to the world in which we live
   C. reconstruction of the total personality and reorganization of the total environment are specific goals
   D. the client is a responsible participant at every step in the solution of his problems

8.____

9. In order to provide those services to problem families which will help restore them to a self-maintaining status, it is necessary to FIRST
   A. develop specific plans to meet the individual needs of the problem family
   B. reduce the size of those caseloads composed of multi-problem families
   C. remove them from their environment and provide them with the means of overcoming their dependency

9.____

D. identify the factors causing their dependency and creating problems for them

10. Of the following, the type of service which can provide the client with the MOST enduring help is that service which
    A. provides him with material aid and relieves the stress of his personal problems
    B. assists him to do as much as he can for himself and leave him free to make his own decisions
    C. directs his efforts towards returning to a self-maintaining status and provides him with desirable goals
    D. gives him the feeling that the agency is interested in him as an individual and stands ready to assist him with his problems

10.____

11. When a client is faced with a new situation which he does not fully understand or know how to handle, the worker can help the client MOST by first
    A. sharing with the client his knowledge of how other people handled similar situations
    B. making the client aware of the facts and possibilities of the situation
    C. explaining to the client what steps he should not take to correct the situation
    D. referring the client to that agency which is best equipped to aid him with his special problem

11.____

12. Psychiatric interpretation of unconscious motivations can bring childhood conflicts into the framework of adult understanding and open the way for them to be resolved, but the interpretation must come from within the client.
    This statement means MOST NEARLY that
    A. treatment is merely diagnosis in reverse
    B. explaining a client to himself will lead to the resolution of his problems
    C. the client must arrive at an understanding of his problems
    D. unresolved childhood conflicts create problems for the adult

12.____

13. When a worker attempts to manipulate a client's environment, he is trying to
    A. rearrange the external situation in order to reduce stress for the client
    B. change the client's emotional attitudes towards his environment
    C. focus the client's attention on the benefits he may derive from his current environment
    D. reinterpret the client's external situation for him

13.____

14. From the point of view of the caseworker in a public welfare agency, the assignment of welfare clients to different categories of assistance serves to
    A. establish uniform standards of need and factors of eligibility
    B. insure an adequate level of assistance by providing federal grants
    C. provide a source of statistical data from which plans for improved services can be drawn
    D. identify those social and health problems upon which casework services should be focused

14.____

15. A significant factor in the United States economic picture is the state of the labor market.
    Of the following, the MOST important development affecting the labor market has been
    A. an expansion of the national defense effort creating new plant capacity
    B. the general increase in personal income as a result of an increase in overtime pay in manufacturing industries
    C. the growth of manufacturing as a result of automation
    D. a demand for a large number of new jobs resulting from new job applicants as well as from displacement of workers by automation

16. A typical characteristic of the United States population over 65 is that MOST of them
    A. are independent and capable of self-support
    B. live in their own homes but require various supportive services
    C. live in institutions for the aged
    D. require constant medical attention at home or an institution

17. An amendment to the Judiciary Article of the State Constitution established
    A. a unified court system for the entire state with appropriate jurisdictions in each district
    B. a separate court for each category of cases and a separate category of cases for each court
    C. a statewide court for all civil cases and a statewide court for all criminal cases
    D. unification of all courts in the city, leaving the courts in the rest of the state unchanged in jurisdiction

18. Under an amendment to the Judiciary Article of the State Constitution, jurisdiction over cases involving the protection and treatment of persons under 16 years of age is vested in the
    A. County Court
    B. Court of Claims
    C. Supreme Court
    D. Family Court

19. The city agency responsible for social casework services to adolescents referred by the district attorney but not indicted for a crime is the
    A. Parole Commission
    B. Youth Board
    C. Youth Counsel Bureau
    D. Office of Probation

20. The public agency responsible for the rehabilitation of neighborhoods and areas in the city characterized by substandard housing is the
    A. City Housing and Redevelopment Board
    B. State Temporary Housing Rent Commission
    C. City Department of Housing and Buildings
    D. City Planning Commission

21. A client residing in a building in which there has been a general decrease in services may request that his rent be reduced.
The agency which has jurisdiction over such rent reductions is the
   A. Housing and Redevelopment Board
   B. City Rent and Rehabilitation Administration
   C. Department of Buildings
   D. Department of Health

21.____

22. Of the following, the principle involved in the computation of disability benefits under the Workers' Compensation Law is payment of
   A. a lump sum for the loss of a limb or bodily organ, depending on the nature and the extent of the injury
   B. two-thirds of the average weekly wages based on the preceding year, not to exceed a statutory sum per week, and all necessary medical care costs for a period depending on the nature and the extent of the injury
   C. medical care costs for the disabled worker during a specified period after the disability
   D. medical care costs for the disabled worker and payment for support of his immediate family during the period of his disability and inability to work

22.____

23. A wage earner who is disabled by an injury or illness incurred outside his employment may receive cash benefits under the Disability Benefits Law.
Such benefits under this law consist of a weekly payment
   A. covering the cost of medical care for the employee and support of his dependents
   B. of half of his current weekly salary plus the cost of medical care as specified by statute
   C. of half of the average weekly wages based on the last 8 weeks of employment
   D. of two-thirds of the average weekly wages based on the past year of employment

23.____

24. A worker becomes disabled and is unable to engage in any substantial gainful activity. He applies for benefits under the Social Security Law.
According to the Social Security regulations, his benefit payment would be based on
   A. a pro-rated benefit for him and his dependents based on his current age
   B. a monthly amount depending on the specific limb or bodily organ injured
   C. the length of time he will probably be disabled
   D. a monthly amount equal to the old age insurance benefit he would receive if he were 65

24.____

25. According to the Social Security Law, the eligible dependent wife of a man who is receiving old age benefits is entitled to receive
   A. up to one-half of the husband's monthly benefit payment
   B. a payment of ten percent less than her husband's monthly benefit payment
   C. up to three-fourths of the husband's monthly benefit payment
   D. a payment equal to her husband's monthly benefit payment

25.____

KEY (CORRECT ANSWERS)

1.	C	11.	B
2.	D	12.	C
3.	A	13.	A
4.	D	14.	D
5.	C	15.	D
6.	B	16.	B
7.	C	17.	A
8.	C	18.	D
9.	D	19.	C
10.	B	20.	A

21.	B
22.	B
23.	C
24.	D
25.	A

TEST 2

DIRECTIONS: Each question or incomplete statement is followed by several suggested answers or completions. Select the one that BEST answers the question or completes the statement. *PRINT THE LETTER OF THE CORRECT ANSWER IN THE SPACE AT THE RIGHT.*

1. When the purpose of a client-worker interview is to discuss the factors affecting his eligibility for public assistance, it would be LEAST appropriate to attempt, at the same time, to
   A. discuss with the applicant the reasons for his dependency and his responsibility for his situation
   B. assess with the applicant what he and his family can do about his immediate problem
   C. assist the applicant to use his capacities to solve his problems
   D. explore with the applicant his views about his problems and about his situation

1.____

2. At an intake interview, a client who seems very hesitant about seeking assistance, but who seems to be in need of help, makes several inconsistent statements about matters affecting his eligibility for public assistance. You have attempted, unsuccessfully, to have the inconsistencies clarified.
   Of the following, the BEST action for the worker to take in this situation is to
   A. accept the case but try to clear up the inconsistencies in subsequent interviews
   B. attempt to clarify the statements through other sources before the next interview
   C. overlook the inconsistencies since the client may be frightened away by any attempt to probe
   D. refuse further help to the client until he presents a more realistic picture of his situation

2.____

3. A woman comes to the intake section of the Department of Welfare. The intake worker discovers, fairly early in the interview, that the applicant has come to the wrong agency for the special help she needs.
   For the worker to continue the interview until the applicant has explained her needs is
   A. *advisable*, mainly because the intake worker should create an atmosphere in which the client can talk freely
   B. *inadvisable*, mainly because the applicant will have to tell her story all over again to another agency's intake worker
   C. *advisable*, mainly because the proper referral cannot be made unless the worker has all the pertinent data
   D. *inadvisable*; the applicant should not be permitted to become too deeply involved in telling her story to an agency which cannot help her

3.____

4. A client has been referred to the Department of Welfare by another agency. The intake worker has reviewed the detailed case history forwarded by the referring agency. When the client comes in for his initial interview, he proceeds to go into detail about his past situation.
For the intake worker to allow the client to relate his history at this point is
   A. *inadvisable*, chiefly because allowing the client to give a detailed account of his past would allow him to control the course of the interview
   B. *advisable*, chiefly because the case history may not fully cover some essential areas
   C. *inadvisable*, chiefly because the facts are fully recorded and valuable time would be wasted in allowing the client to retell them
   D. *advisable*, chiefly because this will give the client the feeling that the worker is interested in him as an individual

5. The type of case record to be used in a specific case depends on its purpose. If the case record is to serve as the document used to validate the kind of service or the amount and type of assistance to be granted, it is MOST important that the case record be
   A. chronological in form so that events can be seen in the proper perspective
   B. factual and not include the worker's evaluations
   C. organized so that information on continuing needs and services given is quickly available
   D. narrative in form so that the full history of the case can be recorded

6. In handling a case, an investigator should summarize the facts he has gathered and the observations he has made about the family and incorporate this material into a formal social study of the family.
Of the following, the CHIEF advantage of such a practice is that it will provide a(n)
   A. picture of the family on the basis of which evaluations and plans can be made
   B. easily accessible listing of the factors pertaining to eligibility
   C. a simple and uniform method of recording the family's social history
   D. an opportunity for the investigator to record his evaluation of the family's situation

7. An applicant for public assistance tells the worker who is investigating his case that he has always supported himself by doing odd jobs.
While attempting to verify the applicant's history of past maintenance, it is MOST important for the worker to determine, in addition,
   A. how the applicant was able to obtain a sufficient number of odd jobs to support himself
   B. what skills the applicant had that enabled him to obtain these jobs
   C. why the applicant never sought or kept a steady job
   D. whether such jobs are still available as a source of income for the applicant

8. For a worker to make a collateral contact with a client's legally responsible relative when that relative is herself receiving public assistance is
   A. *advisable*, mainly because the relative may be able to assist the client with needed services
   B. *inadvisable*, mainly because he relative is in receipt of assistance and cannot assist the client financially
   C. *advisable*, mainly because the worker may obtain information concerning the relative's eligibility for assistance
   D. *inadvisable*, mainly because any information concerning the relative can be obtained from the other welfare center

8._____

9. An applicant for public assistance tells the worker that her bank savings are exhausted.
   While a bank clearance can verify her statement, it is still important for the worker to see her bankbook CHIEFLY in order to
   A. determine when the account was first opened and the amount of the initial deposit
   B. correlate withdrawals and deposits with the applicant's story of past management
   C. learn if the applicant had closed this account in order to open an account in another bank
   D. verify that the last withdrawal was made before the applicant applied for assistance

9._____

10. An unemployed father on welfare has refused to take a job as laborer because he has enrolled in a Federal Manpower Training course which will enable him to become an electrician's helper. He states that once he has completed the course, he is sure that he can get a job and support his family. However, you learn that because of the long waiting list for this course, he cannot begin classes for four months.
    For his refusal to accept this laborer's job to be treated as a job refusal is
    A. *proper*; there is no guarantee that he will be able to obtain employment when he has completed the course
    B. *improper*; he should be encouraged to engage in a training program which will increase his job skills and earning capacity
    C. *proper*; his working as laborer will not interfere with his starting the training course when he is reached
    D. *improper*; he has a right to refuse a low-paying job in view of his potential skills

10._____

11. Because of the heavy load of mail at Christmas time, a welfare family's check has not arrived on the expected date. The investigator visits the family and finds that they are without food or funds.
    For the investigator to ask the local grocer to extend credit to this family until their check arrives is
    A. *advisable*, mainly because the family's need will be met and there will be no need to duplicate assistance.

11._____

B. *inadvisable*, mainly because the worker is sanctioning the family's use of credit buying and this might encourage them to make larger purchases on credit
C. *advisable*, mainly because this is the simplest and fastest way of meeting the family's needs, and the debt can be repaid when the check arrives
D. *inadvisable*, mainly because the family may not repay the debt when they receive their check, and the grocer might sue the worker

12. When the case of an applicant who lives in a Housing Authority project has been accepted, the Housing Authority should be notified of the case acceptance CHIEFLY in order to ensure that the
    A. special services available to Housing Authority tenants are utilized
    B. schedule of rents established for welfare recipients is used
    C. family consists of only those people indicated on the welfare application
    D. Housing Authority is informed of the applicant's reduced income

12.____

13. A client who is receiving supplementary assistance tells his worker that he has been offered a higher paying job. He states, however, that he is not sure that he has the skill to handle the increased job responsibilities and asks the worker for advice.
    The worker should
    A. suggest that he take the job because he will then be able to support his family without help from the Department of Welfare
    B. allow the client to make his decision independently since only he can make such a decision
    C. help him to evaluate his level of skill and his ability to accept the new responsibilities
    D. recommend that the client refuse the job because he may not be able to keep it

13.____

14. It has been suggested that all social investigators be kept currently informed about general departmental actions taken, changes in other departmental work units, and new developments of general interest in their department.
    For a welfare department to put this suggestion into effect is GENERALLY
    A. *inadvisable*; social investigators should perform the duties specifically assigned to them and not get involved in matters that do not concern them directly
    B. *advisable*; social investigators may often need to know such information in order to coordinate their work properly with that of other work units
    C. *inadvisable*; changes in other work units have little effect on the work performed by social investigators not assigned to these units
    D. *advisable*; broad knowledge of the activities in any agency tends to improve social work skills

14.____

15. Although there is a normal distinction between the successive ranks of supervision in an agency, the greatest distinction and change in rank occurs, however, when a social investigator becomes a supervisor.
    This is true CHIEFLY because the supervisor

15.____

A. must be better informed than his workers in all aspects of public welfare
B. must learn to assume new and more complex duties
C. becomes responsible for the first time for the job performance of members of the social service staff
D. has greater responsibility and authority than the social investigators under his supervision

16. When an experienced supervisor does not agree personally with some of the procedurally correct objectives and directions of his supervisor, it would be MOST correct for him to
    A. continue to supervise his unit in accordance with the supervisor's directions
    B. direct his workers to follow the supervisor's directions, but indicate the weaknesses therein and be somewhat more lenient in the supervision of these duties
    C. seek to change the supervisor's directions through use of these duties
    D. develop his own methods and apply them to the work of his unit on a trial basis

16.____

17. It has been said that the success or failure of the work of his unit rests on the unit supervisor.
    If the supervisor wants to stimulate growth among his workers, it would generally be BEST for him to
    A. set an easy pace for his workers so that they will not become confused because of having to learn too much too rapidly
    B. set the pace for his workers so that the job is never too easy but is a constant challenge calling for more and better work
    C. spot check the workers' case records at irregular intervals in order to determine whether they are performing their duties properly
    D. see to it that the broad objectives and goals of the department are periodically communicated and interpreted to his workers

17.____

18. The effectiveness of the work of a unit of social investigators depends in a large measure on that unit's will to work.
    The BEST of the following methods for the unit supervisor to employ in order to increase the will of the member of the unit to work is for the unit supervisor to
    A. allow each worker to proceed at his own pace
    B. be constantly on guard for any laxity among his workers
    C. provide comfortable working facilities for his workers
    D. clearly discuss with his workers the functions and objectives of the agency

18.____

19. For a supervisor to encourage his workers to think about the reasons for a policy is
    A. *advisable*, mainly because the workers are then more likely to apply the policy appropriately
    B. *inadvisable*, mainly because the workers may then apply the policy too flexibly

19.____

C. *advisable*, mainly because the workers then feel that they have participated in policy making
D. *inadvisable*, mainly because the workers may interpret the policy incorrectly if they misunderstand its meaning

20. A supervisor who plans his work properly and who has no difficulty in meeting deadlines insists that his new workers pattern their activities after his in every detail.
    This method is
    A. *undesirable*, chiefly because such compliance can cause antagonism and hamper the workers' growth
    B. *undesirable*, chiefly because this method cannot work as successfully for the new workers
    C. *desirable*, chiefly because the supervisor's methods have proved successful and will eliminate waste
    D. *desirable*, chiefly because the untrained worker needs guidelines to follow

20.____

KEY (CORRECT ANSWERS)

1.	A	11.	D
2.	B	12.	B
3.	C	13.	C
4.	D	14.	B
5.	C	15.	D
6.	A	16.	A
7.	D	17.	B
8.	A	18.	D
9.	B	19.	A
10.	C	20.	A

INTERVIEWING
EXAMINATION SECTION
TEST 1

DIRECTIONS: Each question or incomplete statement is followed by several suggested answers or completions. Select the one that BEST answers the question or completes the statement. *PRINT THE LETTER OF THE CORRECT ANSWER IN THE SPACE AT THE RIGHT.*

1. Of the methods given below for obtaining desired information from applicants, the one considered the BEST interviewing method is to
   A. work from an outline, asking the questions in the order in which they appear and requiring the applicant to give specific answers
   B. let the applicant tell what he has to say in his own way first, the interviewer then taking responsibility for asking questions on points not covered
   C. tell the applicant all the facts that it is necessary to have, then letting him give the information in any way he chooses
   D. verify all such facts as birth date, income, and past employment before seeing the applicant, then asking the applicant to fill in the remaining gaps when he is interviewed

1.____

2. Suppose an applicant objects to answering a question regarding his recent employment and asks, "What business is it of yours, young man?"
   In conducting the interview, the MOST constructive course of action for you to take under the circumstances would be to
   A. tell the applicant you have no intention of prying into his personal affairs and go on to the next question
   B. refer the applicant to your supervisor
   C. rephrase the question so that only a "Yes" or "No" answer is required
   D. explain why the question is being asked

2.____

3. An interview is BEST conducted in private PRIMARILY because
   A. the person interviewed will tend to be less self-conscious
   B. the interviewer will be able to maintain his continuity of thought better
   C. it will insure that the interview is "off the record"
   D. people tend to "show off" before an audience

3.____

4. An interviewer will be better able to understand the person interviewed and his problems if he recognizes that much of the person's behavior is due to motives
   A. which are deliberate   B. of which he is unaware
   C. which are inexplicable   D. which are kept under control

4.____

5. When an applicant is repeatedly told that "everything will be all right," the effect that can USUALLY be expected is that he will
   A. develop overt negativistic reactions toward the agency
   B. become too closely identified with the interviewer
   C. doubt the interviewer's ability to understand and help with his problems
   D. have greater confidence in the interviewer

6. While interviewing a client, it is PREFERABLE that the interviewer
   A. take no notes in order to avoid disturbing the client
   B. focus primary attention on the client while the client is talking
   C. take no notes in order to impress upon the client the interviewer's ability to remember all the pertinent facts of his case
   D. record all the details in order to show the client that what he says is important

7. During an interview, a curious applicant asks several questions about the interviewer's private life.
   As the interviewer, you should
   A. refuse to answer such questions
   B. answer his questions fully
   C. explain that your primary concern is with his problems and that discussion of your personal affairs will not be helpful in meeting his needs
   D. explain that it is the responsibility of the interviewer to ask questions and not to answer them

8. An interviewer can BEST establish a good relationship with the person being interviewed by
   A. assuming casual interest in the statements made by the person being interviewed
   B. asking questions which enable the person to show pride in his knowledge
   C. taking the point of view of the person interviewed
   D. showing a genuine interest in the person

9. An interviewer's attention must be directed toward himself as well as toward the person interviewed.
   This statement means that the interviewer should
   A. keep in mind the extent to which his own prejudices may influence his judgment
   B. rationalize the statements made by the person interviewed
   C. gain the respect and confidence of the person interviewed
   D. avoid being too impersonal

10. More complete expression will be obtained from a person being interviewed if the interviewer can create the impression that
    A. the data secured will become part of a permanent record
    B. official information must be accurate in every detail
    C. it is the duty of the person interviewed to give accurate data
    D. the person interviewed is participating in a discussion of his own problems

11. The practice of asking leading questions should be avoided in an interview because the
    A. interviewer risks revealing his attitudes to the person being interviewed
    B. interviewer may be led to ignore the objective attitudes of the person interviewed
    C. answers may be unwarrantedly influenced
    D. person interviewed will resent the attempt to lead him and will be less cooperative

11._____

12. A good technique for the interviewer to use in an effort to secure reliable data and to reduce the possibility of misunderstanding is to
    A. use casual undirected conversation, enabling the person being interviewed to talk about himself, and thus secure the desired information
    B. adopt the procedure of using direct questions regularly
    C. extract the desired information from the person being interviewed by putting him on the defensive
    D. explain to the person being interviewed the information desired and the reason for needing it

12._____

13. In interviewing an applicant, your attitude toward his veracity should be that the information he has furnished you is
    A. *untruthful* until you have had an opportunity to check the information
    B. *truthful* only insofar as verifiable facts are concerned
    C. *untruthful* because clients tend to interpret everything in their own favor
    D. *truthful* until you have information to the contrary

13._____

14. When an agency assigns its most experienced interviewers to conduct initial interviews with applicants, the MOST important reason for its action is that
    A. experienced workers are always older and, therefore, command the respect of applicants
    B. the applicant may be given a complete understanding of the procedures to be followed and the time involved in obtaining assistance
    C. applicants with fraudulent intentions will be detected, and prevented from obtaining further services from the agency
    D. the applicant may be given an understanding of the purpose of the assistance program and of the bases for granting assistance, in addition to the routine information

14._____

15. In conducting the first interview with an applicant, you should
    A. ask questions requiring "Yes" or "No" answers in order to simplify the interview
    B. rephrase several of the key questions as a check on his previous statements
    C. let him tell his own story while keeping him to the relevant facts
    D. avoid showing any sympathy for the applicant while he is revealing his personal needs and problems

15._____

16. When an interview opens an interview by asking the client direct questions about his work, it is very likely that the client will feel
    A. that the interview is interested in him
    B. at ease if his work has been good
    C. free to discuss his attitudes toward his work
    D. that good reports are of great importance to the interviewer in his thinking

    16._____

17. When an interviewer does NOT understand the meaning of a response that a client has made, the interviewer should
    A. proceed to another topic
    B. state that he does not understand and ask for clarification
    C. act as if he understands so that the client's confidence in him should not be shaken
    D. ask the client to rephrase his response

    17._____

18. When an interviewer makes a response which brings on a high degree of resistance in the client, he should
    A. apologize and rephrase his remark in a less evocative manner
    B. accept the resistance on the part of the client
    C. ignore the client's resistance
    D. recognize that little more will be accomplished in the interview and suggest another appointment

    18._____

19. Most definitions of interviewing would NOT include the following as a necessary aspect:
    A. The interviewer and client meet face-to-face and talk things out
    B. The client is experiencing considerable emotional disturbance
    C. A valuable learning opportunity is provided for the client
    D. The interviewer brings a special competence to the relationship

    19._____

20. A powerful dynamic in the interviewing process and often the very *antonym* of its counterpart in the instructional process is
    A. encouraging accuracy
    B. emphasizing structure
    C. pointing up sequential and orderly thinking
    D. processing ambiguity and equivocation

    20._____

21. Interviewing techniques are frequently useful in working with clients. A basic fundamental is an atmosphere which may BEST be described as
    A. non-threatening
    B. motivating for creativity
    C. highly charged to stimulate excitement
    D. fairly-well structured

    21._____

22. In interviewing the disadvantaged client, the subtle technique of steering away from high-level educational and vocational plans must be *replaced* by
    A. a wait-and-see explanation to the client
    B. the use of prediction tables to determine possibilities and probabilities of overcoming this condition

    22._____

C. avoidance in discussing controversial issues of deprivation
D. encouragement and concrete consideration for planning his future

23. The process of collecting, analyzing, synthesizing, and interpreting information about the client should be
    A. completed prior to interviewing
    B. completed early in the interviewing process
    C. limited to a type of interviewing which is primarily diagnostic in purpose
    D. continuously pursued throughout interviewing

24. Catharsis, the "emotional unloading" of the client's feelings, has a value in the early stages of interviewing because it accomplishes all BUT which one of the following goals?
    It
    A. relieves strong physiological tensions in the client
    B. increases the client's anxiety and aggrandizes his motivation to continue counseling
    C. provides a strong substitute for "acting out" the client's feelings
    D. releases emotional energy which the client has been using to bulwark his defenses

25. In the interviewing process, the interviewer should *usually* give information
    A. whenever it is needed
    B. at the end of the process
    C. in the introductory interview
    D. just before the client would ordinarily request it

KEY (CORRECT ANSWERS)

1.	B		11.	C
2.	D		12.	D
3.	A		13.	D
4.	B		14.	D
5.	C		15.	C
6.	B		16.	D
7.	C		17.	B
8.	D		18.	B
9.	A		19.	B
10.	D		20.	D

21. A
22. D
23. D
24. B
25. A

TEST 2

DIRECTIONS: Each question or incomplete statement is followed by several suggested answers or completions. Select the one that BEST answers the question or completes the statement. *PRINT THE LETTER OF THE CORRECT ANSWER IN THE SPACE AT THE RIGHT.*

1. Of the following problems that might affect the conduct and outcome of an interview, the MOST troublesome and usually the MOST difficult for the interviewer to control is the
    A. tendency of the interviewee to anticipate the needs and preferences of the interviewer
    B. impulse to cut the interviewee off when he seems to have reached the end of an idea
    C. tendency of interviewee attitude to bias the results
    D. tendency of the interviewer to do most of the talking

    1.____

2. The supervisor MOST likely to be a good interviewer is one who
    A. is adept at manipulating people and circumstances toward his objective
    B. is able to put himself in the position of the interviewee
    C. gets the more difficult questions out of the way at the beginning of the interview
    D. develops one style and technique that can be used in any type of interview

    2.____

3. A good interviewer guards against the tendency to form an overall opinion about an interviewee on the basis of a single aspect of the interviewee's makeup.
    This statement refers to a well-known source of error in interviewing known as the
    A. assumption error
    B. expectancy error
    C. extension effect
    D. halo effect

    3.____

4. In conducting an "exit interview" with an employee who is leaving voluntarily, the interview's MAIN objective should be to
    A. see that the employee leaves with a good opinion of the organization
    B. learn the true reasons for the employee's resignation
    C. find out if the employee would consider a transfer
    D. try to get the employee to remain on the job

    4.____

5. During an interview, an interviewee unexpectedly discloses a relevant but embarrassing personal fact.
    It would be BEST for the interviewer to
    A. listen calmly, avoiding any gesture or facial expression that would suggest approval or disapproval of what is related
    B. change the subject, since further discussion in this area may reveal other embarrassing, but irrelevant, personal facts

    5.____

C. apologize to the interviewee for having led him to reveal such a fact and promise not to do so again
D. bring the interview to a close as quickly as possible in order to avoid a discussion which may be distressing to the interviewee

6. Suppose that, while you are interviewing an applicant for a position in your office, you notice a contradiction in facts in two of his responses.
For you to call the contradictions to his attention would be
   A. *inadvisable*, because it reduces the interviewee's level of participation
   B. *advisable*, because getting the facts is essential to a successful interview
   C. *inadvisable*, because the interviewer should use more subtle techniques to resolve any discrepancies
   D. *advisable*, because the interviewee should be impressed with the necessity for giving consistent answers

7. An interviewer should be aware that an undesirable result of including "leading questions" in an interview is to
   A. cause the interviewee to give a "yes" or "no" answers with qualification or explanation
   B. encourage the interviewee to discuss irrelevant topics
   C. encourage the interviewee to give more meaningful information
   D. reduce the validity of the information obtained from the interviewee

8. The kind of interview which is particularly helpful in getting an employee to tell about his complaints and grievances is one in which
   A. a pattern has been worked out involving a sequence of exact questions to be asked
   B. the interviewee is expected to support his statements with specific evidence
   C. the interviewee is not made to answer specific questions but is encouraged to talk freely
   D. the interviewer has specific items on which he wishes to get or give information

9. Suppose you are scheduled to interview an employee under your supervision concerning a health problem. You know that some of the questions you will be asking him will seem embarrassing to him, and that he may resist answering these questions.
In general, to hold these questions for the last part of the interview would be
   A. *desirable*; the intervening time period gives the interviewer an opportunity to plan how to ask these sensitive questions.
   B. *undesirable*; the employee will probably feel that he has been tricked when he suddenly must answer embarrassing questions
   C. *desirable*; the employee will probably have increased confidence in the interviewer and be more willing to answer these questions
   D. *undesirable*; questions that are important should not be deferred until the end of the interview

3 (#2)

10. In conducting an interview, the BEST types of questions with which to begin the interview are those which the person interviewed is
    A. willing and able to answer
    B. willing but unable to answer
    C. able but unwilling to answer
    D. unable and unwilling to answer

11. In order to determine accurately a child's age, it is BEST for an interviewer to rely on
    A. the child's grade in school
    B. what the mother says
    C. birth records
    D. a library card

12. In his first interview with a new employee, it would be LEAST appropriate for a unit supervisor to
    A. find out the employee's preference for the several types of jobs to which he is able to assign him
    B. determine whether the employee will make good promotion material
    C. inform the employee of what his basic job responsibilities will be
    D. inquire about the employee's education and previous employment

13. If an interviewer takes care to phrase his questions carefully and precisely, the result will MOST probably be that
    A. he will be able to determine whether the person interviewed is being truthful
    B. the free flow of the interview will be lost
    C. he will get the information he wants
    D. he will ask stereotyped questions and narrow the scope of the interview

14. When, during an interview, is the person interviewed LEAST likely to be cautious about what he tells the interviewer?
    A. Shortly after the beginning when the questions normally suggest pleasant associations to the person interviewed
    B. As long as the interviewer keeps his questions to the point
    C. At the point where the person interviewed gains a clear insight into the area being discussed
    D. When the interview appears formally ended and goodbyes are being said

15. In an interview held for the purpose of getting information from the person interviewed, it is sometimes desirable for the interviewer to repeat the answer he has received to a question.
    For the interviewer to rephrase such an answer in his own words is good practice MAINLY because it
    A. gives the interviewer time to make up his next question
    B. gives the person interviewed a chance to correct any possible misunderstanding
    C. gives the person interviewed the feeling that the interviewer considers his answer important
    D. prevents the person interviewed from changing his answer

16. There are several methods of formulating questions during an interview. The particular method used should be adapted to the interview problems presented by the person being questioned.
    Of the following methods of formulating questions during an interview, the ACCEPTABLE one is for the interviewer to ask questions which
    A. incorporate several items in order to allow a cooperative interviewee freedom to organize his statements
    B. are ambiguous in order to foil a distrustful interviewee
    C. suggest the correct answer in order to assist an interviewee who appears confused
    D. would help an otherwise unresponsive interviewee to become more responsive

17. For an interviewer to permit the person being interviewed to read the data the interviewer writes as he records the person's responses on a routine departmental form is
    A. *desirable*, because it serves to assure the person interviewed that his responses are being recorded accurately
    B. *undesirable*, because it prevents the interviewer from clarifying uncertain points by asking additional questions
    C. *desirable*, because it makes the time that the person interviewed must wait while the answer is written seem shorter
    D. *undesirable*, because it destroys the confidentiality of the interview

18. Of the following methods of conducting an interview, the BEST is to
    A. ask questions with "yes" or "no" answers
    B. listen carefully and ask only questions that are pertinent
    C. fire questions at the interviewee so that he must answer sincerely and briefly
    D. read standardized questions to the person being interviewed

KEY (CORRECT ANSWERS)

1.	A	11.	C
2.	B	12.	B
3.	D	13.	C
4.	B	14.	D
5.	A	15.	B
6.	B	16.	D
7.	D	17.	A
8.	C	18.	B
9.	C		
10.	A		

EXAMINATION SECTION
TEST 1

DIRECTIONS: Each question or incomplete statement is followed by several suggested answers or completions. Select the one that BEST answers the question or completes the statement. *PRINT THE LETTER OF THE CORRECT ANSWER IN THE SPACE AT THE RIGHT.*

1. Which of the following provides the BEST rationale for increased government involvement in solving current urban problems?
    A. The cities are not so badly off as they seem to be.
    B. Additional research and experimentation is needed to develop solutions to urban problems.
    C. Our current urban problems have obvious and simple solutions.
    D. The only thing that prevents us from solving urban problems is public opinion.

1.____

2. Ethnic identity as a factor in urban America
    A. has virtually disappeared with the rapid assimilation of second and third generation immigrants
    B. has little influence on patterns of occupational mobility
    C. has become an increasingly important determinant of residential choices
    D. continues to exercise an influence on voting behavior

2.____

3. In recent years, there has been a move to decentralize the governmental structure of some of our largest cities.
   The one of the following which provides the WEAKEST argument in favor of decentralization is that decentralization will help to
    A. increase administrative responsiveness to neighborhood needs
    B. promote local democracy by developing local leaders
    C. diminish conflict between communities
    D. develop community cohesion

3.____

4. The decentralization and diffusion of metropolitan areas has resulted in
    A. a dramatic decline in the overall population density of the central city
    B. spatial segregation on the basis of race, ethnicity, and class
    C. slow-down in the rate of suburban growth in comparison to central city growth
    D. benefit to persons from lower socio-economic levels by reducing the population density of the poorest sections of the central city

4.____

5. The concentration of the poor in the core areas of the modern decentralized metropolis can BEST be explained by the
    A. failure of public transport systems to follow the new multi-centered pattern of commercial and industrial dispersion
    B. absence of low-skilled jobs in outlying industrial and commercial sub centers

5.____

C. availability of inexpensive goods and services in the central city
D. need such people feel for the security of familiar surroundings

6. Of the following, the MOST serious shortcoming of urban renewal has been that it has
   A. not attempted to modernize aging downtown areas
   B. curtailed industrial and commercial expansion in the cities
   C. failed to provide adequate housing for poor families forced to move out of their old neighborhoods
   D. not stimulated public support for public housing appropriations

6.____

7. The vast majority of blacks who had migrated from the South to northern cities had done so PRIMARILY in order to
   A. join friends and relatives
   B. take specific jobs or look for work
   C. take advantage of superior educational facilities
   D. escape southern racial prejudices

7.____

8. The one of the following that is the CHIEF justification for developing area-wide planning in health care is that such planning is likely to
   A. promote effective use of a community's total health resources
   B. minimize the need for consumer participation
   C. reduce the total cost of medical care in a community
   D. reduce the number of physicians needed in a community

8.____

9. Of the following, the CHIEF reason that the gridiron design, which consists of straight vertical streets that lie perpendicular to horizontal streets, became the dominant planning motif in urban America is that it
   A. facilitated the movement of automobile traffic to central locations
   B. was a convenient and efficient form of subdividing real estate to maximize its utilization
   C. provided fixed boundaries for neighborhoods
   D. could be easily adapted to topographical variations

9.____

10. Which of the following is generally the LARGEST cost factor in acquiring and owning a home?
    A. Building materials
    B. Skilled labor
    C. Interest on mortgage
    D. Builder's profit

10.____

11. The federally funded job training programs of the 1960's were INITIALLY conceived on the assumption that
    A. the unemployed lacked the necessary skills to qualify for existing job vacancies
    B. people who dropped out of the labor force lost their motivation to work
    C. public assistance made low wage jobs unattractive to the unemployed
    D. the unemployed would not take menial jobs

11.____

12. Which of the following statements about the urban poor is ACCURATE? 12.____
    A. The proportion of poor people in central cities is the same as in suburbs.
    B. Persons under the age of eighteen constitute the largest group of poor persons.
    C. The number of poor persons living in households headed by women has declined.
    D. The majority of poor persons are in households headed by men under the age of sixty-five.

13. Which one of the following statements concerning health care in America is CORRECT? 13.____
    A. All accepted indices indicate that our general health status is higher than that of other countries.
    B. The quality of our doctors and nurses is higher than in other countries.
    C. All people have equal access to the same quality of such care.
    D. The cost of the same quality of care is lower than in most other countries.

14. Of the following, the MOST serious shortcoming of low income public housing sponsored by the federal government is that 14.____
    A. income limitations are imposed upon the tenants
    B. housing administrators place too few restrictions on tenant activities
    C. it competes with the private housing market
    D. it has been built primarily in old and dilapidated neighborhoods

15. Which of the following is the LEAST important factor contributing to the residential segregation of blacks in metropolitan areas? 15.____
    A. Violence against the black renter and homeowner in white neighborhoods
    B. Fear by whites that the economic value of their property will decline if blacks move into white neighborhoods
    C. Personal preferences of blacks and whites
    D. Fear by whites that the quality of schools will decline if blacks move into white neighborhoods

16. Which of the following is the MOST regressive form of local taxation? _____ tax. 16.____
    A. General sales   B. Property
    C. Personal income   D. Corporate income

17. The property tax has come under attack in metropolitan regions because 17.____
    A. it fails to discriminate between different types of property within a single taxing jurisdiction
    B. insufficient revenues are raised by the tax
    C. it fails to tax improvements in property
    D. the same type of property is taxed at different rates in different communities within a region

18. Advocates of the culture of poverty hypothesis maintain that remedial action should center on the
    A. discriminatory practices against minorities
    B. lack of work opportunity
    C. attitudes and behavior of the poor
    D. inequitable distribution of educational facilities

    18.____

19. The one of the following statements concerning crime in our large cities which is LEAST accurate is that
    A. the readily availability of valuable goods in our affluent society has contributed to the increase in crime
    B. young people have a higher crime rate than adults
    C. the increased ability of poor persons to move about the city has contributed to the increase in crime
    D. murder, rape, and aggravated assault constitute the majority of serious crimes as defined by the F.B.I.'s Uniform Crime Reports

    19.____

20. In assessing the impact of the automobile and public mass transportation on urban population congestion, it is MOST accurate to state that
    A. the construction of an elaborate metropolitan expressway system will relieve such congestion
    B. neither the automobile nor public mass transportation can relieve such congestion
    C. adequate knowledge about the relationship between such congestion and various modes of transportation is still lacking
    D. both the automobile and public mass transportation promote such congestion

    20.____

21. The Supreme Court, in March 1973, reversed previous lower court decisions which had tried to establish that the financing of education through local property taxes was unconstitutional.
    These lower court decisions were based on the contention that
    A. the property tax was applied inequitably in certain areas
    B. the property tax is not an important source of local revenues
    C. the quality of a child's education was dependent on the wealth of the community
    D. districts with a small tax base would have to add a *value added tax*

    21.____

22. The percentage of local revenues which is spent on schools is smaller in urban communities than it is in suburban communities PRIMARILY because
    A. the need for quality education is not as well recognized in urban communities
    B. the tax base of urban communities is insufficient
    C. other public services in urban communities absorb a larger proportion of available funds
    D. commercial enterprises do not pay school taxes

    22.____

23. The one of the following which BEST describes the trend of the drop-out rate in public high schools during the last five years is that this rate
    A. rose sharply
    B. showed little fluctuation throughout the period and ended at the same level this year as it was five years ago
    C. declined sharply
    D. showed considerable fluctuation throughout the period and ended at the same level this year as it was five years ago

23._____

24. One of the findings of the Coleman Report, EQUALITY OF EDUCATIONAL OPPORTUNITY, was that the degree to which black students felt they could affect their environment and future is related to their achievement AND to the
    A. quality of the teaching staff
    B. number of college preparatory courses offered at the high school level
    C. condition of physical facilities
    D. proportion of whites in the school

24._____

25. The concept of cultural pluralism is MOST actively opposed by
    A. the Amish
    B. supporters of black studies as a discipline
    C. supporters of bilingual education
    D. supporters of parochial schools

25._____

KEY (CORRECT ANSWERS)

1.	B		11.	A
2.	D		12.	B
3.	C		13.	B
4.	D		14.	D
5.	A		15.	A
6.	C		16.	A
7.	B		17.	D
8.	A		18.	C
9.	B		19.	D
10.	C		20.	C

21.	C
22.	C
23.	A
24.	D
25.	A

TEST 2

DIRECTIONS: Each question or incomplete statement is followed by several suggested answers or completions. Select the one that BEST answers the question or completes the statement. *PRINT THE LETTER OF THE CORRECT ANSWER IN THE SPACE AT THE RIGHT.*

1. When police provide patrol services on the basis of workload, a high concentration of patrol officers in minority group neighborhoods often results. The police then are subject to criticism both from minority residents who feel persecuted by the police and from residents of other neighborhoods who feel they are not receiving the same level of police protection.
Which one of the following BEST states both whether or not, under these conditions, patrol distribution should be changed and also the BEST reason therefor?
It should
   A. *not be changed*, because community pressure should not be allowed to influence police decisions
   B. *be changed*, because all neighborhoods in the community are entitled to the same level of police protection
   C. *be changed*, because it is necessary for the police to respond to community pressures in order to improve community relations
   D. *not be changed*, because having police concentration in minority neighborhoods protects the remainder of the community from riot situations
   E. *not be changed*, because to do so would deprive law-abiding minority neighborhood residents of police protection to their need

1._____

2. A certain boy is raised by parents who are concerned with status, social position the *right* occupation, the *right* friends, the *right* neighborhood, etc. Social behavior plays a vital role in their lives, and their outlook with regard to rearing children can best be summed up by *children should be seen and not heard*. Following are four descriptive terms their son might possibly be likely to use if he were asked to describe the *perfect boy*:
   I. Being polite   II. Being a good companion
   III. Being clean   IV. Being fun
Which one of the following choices MOST accurately classifies the above statements into those the boy is MOST likely to use when describing the *perfect boy* and those which he is LEAST likely to use?
He is
   A. most likely to use I and II and least likely to use III and IV
   B. most likely to use I and III and least likely to use II and IV
   C. most likely to use I, II, and III and least likely to use IV
   D. most likely to use II and IV and least likely to use I and III
   E. equally likely to use any of I, II, III, and IV

2._____

3. People adjust to frustrations or conflicts in many different words. One of these ways of adjustment is known as projection.
Which one of the following behaviors is the BEST example of projection?
A person
   A. who is properly arrested for inciting a riot protests against police brutality and violence
   B. stopped for going through a red light claims that he couldn't help it because his brakes wouldn't hold
   C. who is arrested for a crime persistently claims to have forgotten the whole incident that led to his arrest
   D. who is arrested for a crime cries, screams, and stamps his feet on the floor like a child having a temper tantrum
   E. who is stopped for a traffic violation claims that he is a close friend of the mayor in order to escape blame for the violation

3._____

4. A certain police officer was patrolling a playground area where adolescent gangs had been causing troubles and holding drinking parties. He approached a teenage boy who was alone and drinking from a large paper cup. He asked the boy what he was drinking, and the boy replied *Coke*. The officer asked the boy for the cup, and the boy refused to give it to him. The officer then explained that he wanted to check the contents, and the boy still refused to give it to him. The officer then demanded the cup, and the boy reluctantly gave it to him. The officer smelled the contents of the cup and determined that it was, in fact, Coke. He then told the boy to move along and emptied the Coke on the ground.
Which one of the following is the MOST serious error, if any, made by the officer in handling this situation?
   A. The officer should not have made any effort to determine what was in the cup.
   B. The officer should not have explained to the boy why he wanted to have the cup.
   C. The officer should have returned the Coke to the boy and allowed the boy to stay where he was.
   D. The officer should have first placed the boy under arrest before taking the cup from him.
   E. None of the above since the officer made no error in handling the situation.

4._____

5. Sociological studies have revealed a great deal of information about the behavior and characteristics of homosexuals.
Which one of the following statements about male homosexuals is MOST accurate?
   A. Male homosexual activity is engaged in by less than 10% of the population.
   B. Most male homosexuals would like to be cured if it were possible.
   C. Male homosexuals are more likely than other sex deviates to commit assaults on female children.
   D. Most male homosexuals pose a threat to the morals and safety of a community and should be removed from the streets.

5._____

E. Most male homosexuals pose no threat to a community and are content to restrict their activities to people of similar tastes.

6. Which one of the following is the MOST important factor for the police department to consider in building a good public image?
   A. A good working relationship with the news media
   B. An efficient police-community relations program
   C. An efficient system for handling citizen complaints
   D. The proper maintenance of police facilities and equipment
   E. The behavior of individual officers in their contacts with the public

6._____

7. Following are four aspects of Black culture which sociologists and psychologists might possibly consider as health aspects:
   I.   Use of hair straighteners   II. Use of skin bleaches
   III. Use of natural Afro hair styles   IV. Use of African style of dress
   Which one of the following MOST accurately classifies the above into those that sociologists do consider healthy and those that they do not?
   A. I and III are considered healthy, but II and IV are not
   B. I, III, and IV are considered healthy but II is not
   C. None of I, II, III, and IV is considered healthy
   D. III is considered healthy, but I, II, and IV are not
   E. III and IV are considered healthy, but I and II are not

7._____

8. Which one of the following situations is MOST responsible for making police-community relations more difficult in a densely populated, low income precinct?
   A. The majority of residents in such precincts do not want police on patrol in their communities.
   B. Radio patrol car sectors in such precincts are too small to give patrol officers an understanding of community problems
   C. The higher ratio of arrests per capita in such precincts leads law-abiding residents in such a precinct to feel oppressed by police.
   D. Such precincts tend to have little or no communication among residents so efforts to improve police-community relations must be on an individual level.
   E. This type of precinct has a higher rate of crime and, therefore, law-abiding residents are often bitter because they feel the police give them inferior protection.

8._____

9. Research studies based on having children draw pictures of police officers at work have shown that children of low income minority group parents are more likely to see police as aggressive than children of upper-middle class white parents. One police department had a group of low-income children participate in a 20-minute discussion with a police officer, and then allowed the youngsters a chance to sit in a police car, blow the siren, etc.
Which one of the following BEST states what effect, if any, this approach MOST likely had on the pictures drawn by the children when they were released two days later?
   A. The children showed almost no hostility toward police.
   B. The children showed significantly less hostility toward police.

9._____

C. The children showed significantly more hostility toward police.
D. There was essentially no change in the attitudes of the children.
E. The children showed a loss of respect for the police, who saw them as weak and permissive

10. Following are three possible complaints against police which might be made frequently by blacks living in cities where riots have taken place:
   I. Lack of adequate channels for complaints against police officers
   II. Failure of police departments to provide adequate protection for Blacks
   III. Discriminatory police employment or promotional practices with regard to Black officers

   Which one of the following choices MOST accurately classifies the above into those which have been frequent complaints and those which have not?
   A. I is a frequent complaint, but II and III are not.
   B. I and II are frequent complaints, but III is not.
   C. I and III are frequent complaints, but II is not.
   D. All of I, II, and III are frequent complaints.
   E. None of I, II, or III is a frequent complaint.

11. A career criminal is one who actively engages in crime as his lifework. Which one of the following statements about *career criminals* is MOST accurate?
   A *career criminal*
   A. understands that prison is a normal occupational hazard
   B. is very likely to suffer from deep emotional and psychological problems
   C. has a lower average intelligence than the average for the general public
   D. is just as likely to engage in violence during a crime as any other criminal
   E. is less likely to have begun his crime career as a juvenile when compared to other criminals

12. Which one of the following choices BEST describes the tactic of non-violent resistance as used by civil rights groups?
   The
   A. willingness of persons to accept unlawful arrest without resistance
   B. avoiding of prosecution for violations of law by refusing to appear in court when required
   C. teasing and verbal harassment of police officers in order to cause unlawful arrests
   D. intentional violation of a particular law by persons unwilling to accept the penalty for violating that law
   E. intentional violation of a particular law by persons willing to accept the penalty for violating that law

13. Which one of the following is the MOST accurate statement about the civil disorders that occurred in the United States in the first nine months of 1967?
   A. Damage caused by riots was much greater than initial estimates indicated.
   B. They intended to be unplanned outbursts, not events planned by militants or agitators.

C. The principal targets of attack were homes, schools, and businesses owned by Black merchants.
D. There were very few minor riots; either there were major riots or there were no riots.
E. The majority of persons killed or injured in the disorders were police officers and white civilians.

14. Some managers try to achieve goals by manipulating or deceiving subordinates into doing what the managers want. Such a manager normally is motivated by a desire to control people or by a desire to hide his own inadequacies. Such a manager also wants to hide the reasons for his actions from those he manages. This type of manager is often referred to as a *facade builder*. Which one of the following types of behavior is LEAST characteristic of this type of manager.
He
   A. shows concern for other people
   B. avoids criticizing other people
   C. gives praise and approval easily
   D. delegates responsibility for administering punishment
   E. avoids getting involved in internal conflicts within the organization

14.____

15. Which one of the following choices states both the MOST PROBABLE effect on crime rate statistics of increased public confidence in police and also the MOST IMPORTANT reason for this effect?
   A. The overall statistical crime rate would decrease because people would be less likely to commit crimes.
   B. The overall statistical crime rate would increase because people would be more likely to report crimes.
   C. The overall statistical crime rate would increase because police would probably be clearing more crimes by arrest.
   D. The overall statistical crime rate would decrease because police would be less likely to arrest offender for minor violations.
   E. Increased public confidence in police would have no effect on the overall statistical crime rate because this depends on the number of crimes committed, not public attitude toward police.

15.____

16. One of the important tasks of any administrator is the development of a proper filing system for classifying written documents by subject.
Following are three suggested rules for subject cross-referencing which might possibly be considered proper:
   I. All filed material should have at least one subject cross-reference.
   II. There should be no limit on the number of subject cross-references that may be made for a single record.
   III. The original document should be filed under the primary classification subject, with only cross-reference sheets, not considered as records, being filed under the cross-reference subject classifications.

16.____

Which one of the following choices MOST accurately classifies the above into those that are proper rules for cross-referencing and those that are not?
- A. I is a proper rule, but II and III are not.
- B. I and III are proper rules, but II is not.
- C. II and III are proper rules, but I is not
- D. III is a proper rule, but I and II are not.
- E. None of I, II, and III is a proper rule.

17. Wherever gambling, prostitution, and narcotics distribution openly flourish, they are usually accompanied by community charges of *protection* on the part of local police.
    Which one of the following BEST states both whether or not such changes have merit and also the BEST reason therefor?
    The charges
    - A. *do not have, merit* because the nature of these operations makes them very difficult to detect
    - B. *have merit*, because such operations cannot long continue openly without some measure of police protection
    - C. *have merit*, because offenses of this type are among the easiest to eliminate
    - D. *do not have merit*, because the local patrol forces probably do not have responsibility for large-scale vice enforcement
    - E. *do not have merit*, because vice flourishes openly only in a community which desires it; therefore, it is the community that is providing the protection

17.____

18. The PRIMARY function of a department of social services is to
    - A. refer needy persons to legally responsible relatives for support
    - B. enable needy persons to become self-supporting
    - C. refer ineligible persons to private agencies
    - D. grant aid to needy eligible persons
    - E. administer public assistance programs in which the federal and state governments do not participate

18.____

19. A public assistance program objective should be designed to
    - A. provide for eligible persons in accordance with their individual requirements and with consideration of the circumstances in which they live
    - B. provide for eligible persons at a standard of living equal to that enjoyed while they were self-supporting
    - C. make sure that assistance payments from public funds are not too liberal
    - D. guard against providing a better living for persons receiving aid than is enjoyed by the most frugal independent families
    - E. eliminate the need for private welfare agencies

19.____

20. It is often stated that it would be better to abolish the need for relief rather than to extend the existing public assistance programs.

20.____

This statement suggests that
- A. existing legislation makes it too easy for people to apply for and receive assistance
- B. public assistance should be limited to institutional care for rehabilitative purposes
- C. the support of needy persons should be the responsibility of their own families and relatives rather than that of the government
- D. the existing criteria used to determine *need* for public assistance are too liberal and should be modified to include a *work test*
- E. attempts should be made to eradicate those forces in our social organization which cause poverty

21. The one of the following types of public assistance which is FREQUENTLY described as a *special privilege* is
    - A. veteran assistance
    - B. emergency assistance
    - C. aid to dependent children
    - D. old-age assistance
    - E. vocational rehabilitation of the handicapped

22. The principle of *settlement* holds that each community is responsible for the care of its own members and that communities should not bear the costs of care for needy non-residents.
    This was an intrinsic principle of the
    - A. English Poor Laws
    - B. Home Rule Amendment
    - C. Single Tax Proposal
    - D. National Bankruptcy Regulations
    - E. Proportional Representation Act

23. The FIRST form of state social security legislation developed in the United States was
    - A. health insurance
    - B. unemployment compensation
    - C. workmen's compensation
    - D. old-age insurance
    - E. old-age assistance

24. The plan for establishing a federal government with Cabinet formerly called the Department of Health, Education, and Welfare was
    - A. vetoed by the President after having been passed by Congress
    - B. disapproved by the Senate after having been passed by the House of Representatives
    - C. rejected by both the Senate and the House of Representatives
    - D. enacted into legislation
    - E. determined to be unconstitutional

25. Census Bureau reports show certain definite social trends in our population. One of these trends which was a MAJOR contributing factor in the establishment of the federal old-age insurance system is the
    - A. increased rate of immigration to the United States
    - B. rate at which the number of Americans living to 65 years of age and beyond is increasing

C. increasing amounts spent for categorical relief in the country as a whole
D. decreasing number of legally responsible relatives who have been unable to assist he aged since the depression of 1929
E. number of states which have failed to meet their obligations in the care of the aged

KEY (CORRECT ANSWERS)

1.	E	11.	A
2.	B	12.	E
3.	A	13.	B
4.	C	14.	E
5.	E	15.	B
6.	E	16.	C
7.	E	17.	B
8.	E	18.	D
9.	B	19.	A
10.	D	20.	E

21.	A
22.	A
23.	C
24.	D
25.	B

READING COMPREHENSION
UNDERSTANDING AND INTERPRETING WRITTEN MATERIAL
EXAMINATION SECTION
TEST 1

DIRECTIONS: Each question or incomplete statement is followed by several suggested answers or completions. Select the one that BEST answers the question or completes the statement. *PRINT THE LETTER OF THE CORRECT ANSWER IN THE SPACE AT THE RIGHT.*

Questions 1-8.

DIRECTIONS: Questions 1 through 8 are to be answered on the basis of the following passage.

The child lives in a context which is itself neither simple nor unitary and which continuously affects his behavior and development. Patterns of stimulation come to him out of this context. In turn, by virtue of his own make-up, he selects from that context. At all times, there is a reciprocal relation between the human organism and his biosocial context. Because the child is limited in time, behavior becomes structured, and patterns develop both in the stimulus field and in his own response system. Some stimulus patterns become significant because they modify the developmental stream by affecting practice or social relations with others. Others remain insignificant because they do not affect this web of relations. Why one pattern is significant and another is not is a crucial problem for child psychology.

1. The author states that
    A. environmental forces have an important effect in determining both the child's actions and his course of growth
    B. environmental and hereditary forces play an equal part in determining both the child's actions and his course of growth
    C. even the environmental forces which are not consciously important to the child can affect both learning and personality
    D. the child's personality is shaped more by the total pattern of pressures in the environment

1._____

2. The author develops *context* so as to make it mean
    A. the nature of the child's immediate environment
    B. a complex rather than a simple home structure
    C. a multitude of past, present, and future forces
    D. internal as well as external influences

2._____

3. According to the author, the CRITICAL forces to be studied are those which
    A. are unconscious forces
    B. are conscious, unconscious, and subconscious forces
    C. cause the child to respond
    D. modify the child's interpersonal relationships

3._____

4. The author's point of view might BEST be labeled as   4.____
   A. environmentalist   B. behaviorist
   C. psychobiosocial   D. gestaltist

5. The author maintains that the environment   5.____
   A. is relatively stable
   B. is in a constant state of flux
   C. shows periods of marked instability
   D. is more stable than unstable

6. From the above paragraph, it is to be inferred that the   6.____
   A. child's personality is mechanistically determined by the nature of the environment
   B. unique personality between the child and his environment shapes his personality
   C. child really shapes his own personality
   D. child's personality is more likely to be affected by than to affect the environment

7. By *structured behavior*, the author means   7.____
   A. conditioning of responses
   B. differentiated activity
   C. characteristic modes of reaction
   D. responses that have been modified by the developmental stream

8. The *patterns* to which the author refers are   8.____
   A. different for all children
   B. culturally determined mainly
   C. biologically determined mainly
   D. psychologically determined mainly

Questions 9-13.

DIRECTIONS: Questions 9 through 13 are to be answered on the basis of the following passage.

The Division of Child Guidance makes certain provisions for summer vacations for children receiving foster care. Foster parents wishing to take the child on a vacation within the United States must file Form CG-42 in duplicate at the office of the Division not later than 3 weeks prior to the starting date of the planned vacation. Such request must be approved in writing by the Social Investigator and the Assistant Supervisor. After the request has been approved, the original copy of Form CG-42 must be returned to the foster parents by the Social Investigator no later than 3 days prior to the planned starting date of the vacation. The city continues to pay the foster parents the standard rate for the child's care.

If the foster parents plan to take the child on a vacation outside the continental United States, Form CG-42 must be submitted in triplicate and must be received no later than 5 weeks prior to the starting date of the planned vacation. Such Form CG-42 for vacation outside the country must also be approved by the Case Supervisor. There will be no payment for time spent outside the United States.

When the approved original Form CG-42 is returned to the foster parents, it shall be accompanied by an original copy of Form CG-43. A duplicate copy of Form CG-43 shall be forwarded by the Case Supervisor to the Children's Accounts Section to stop payment for time expected to be spent outside the United States.

9. When a foster parent plans to take his foster child on a vacation trip, the Division of Child Guidance must receive Form 9.____
    A. CG-42 in triplicate no later than five weeks prior to the scheduled start of his vacation trip to Canada
    B. CG-42 in triplicate no later than three weeks prior to the scheduled start of his vacation trip to Mexico
    C. CG-43 in triplicate no later than three weeks prior to the scheduled start of the vacation trip to Arizona
    D. CG-43 in duplicate no later than five weeks prior to the scheduled start of his vacation trip regardless of location

10. The one of the following steps which is required in processing a request from a foster parent to take a child on a vacation trip is that the 10.____
    A. Case Supervisor send the original copy of Form CG-42 to the appropriate section in the case of a child who will spend all his vacation in a foreign country
    B. Children's Accounts Section receive the duplicate copy of Form CG-43 in the case of a child who will spend any part of his vacation in a foreign country
    C. Division of Child Guidance keep a permanent file of original copies of Form CG-43 to keep a control of all current vacation requests
    D. foster parents receive the triplicate copy of Form CG-42 from the Social Investigator in the case of a child who will spend part of his vacation in the United States

11. When a foster child spends an approved vacation with his foster father, payment for the child's care will be given to the foster father for 11.____
    A. none of the time if part of the vacation is spent in a foreign country
    B. that part of the vacation spent inside the United States but a reduced daily rate
    C. the entire period at a standard rate if the vacation is spent wholly in the United States
    D. the entire time regardless of whether or not it is spent in a foreign country

12. The Division of Child Guidance must notify a foster parent that his request to take his foster child on a vacation outside the country has been approved by sending him the approved _____ copy of Form CG-42 and _____ copy of CG-43. 12.____
    A. duplicate; duplicate   B. duplicate; original
    C. original; duplicate   D. original; original

13. On the basis of the above passage, children receiving foster care may be taken on a vacation trip by their foster parents to a location 13._____
    A. anywhere in the world with the written approval of the Social Investigator only
    B. of the foster parents' choosing but only with the written approval of both the Assistant Supervisor and Case Supervisor
    C. outside the United States but only with the written approval of the Social Investigator, Assistant Supervisor, and Case Supervisor
    D. within the United States with the written approval of the Case Supervisor only

Questions 14-18.

DIRECTIONS: Questions 14 through 18 are statements based on the following paragraphs. For each question, there are two statements.
Based on the information in the paragraphs, mark your answer:
A. if only statement I is correct;
B. if only statement II is correct;
C. if both statements are correct.
Mark your answer D if the excerpts do not contain sufficient evidence for concluding whether either or both statements are correct.

Almost 49,000 children were living in foster family homes or voluntary institutions in the state at the end of 2003. These were children whose parents or relatives were unable or unwilling to care for them in their own homes. The State Department of Social Services supervised the care of these children served under the auspices of 64 social services districts and more than 150 private agencies and institutions. Almost 8 out of every 1,000 children 18 years of age or younger were in care away from their homes at the end of 2003. This estimate does not include a substantial, but unknown, number of children living outside their own homes who were placed there by their parents, relatives, or others without the assistance of a social agency.

The number of children in care (dependent, neglected, and delinquent combined) was up by 4,500 or 10 percent over the 2000-2003 period. Both the city and state reported similar increases. In the comparable period, the state's child population (18 years or less) rose only three percent. Thus, the foster care rate showed a moderate increase to 7.7 per thousand in 2003 from 7.2 thousand in 2000. The city's foster care rate in 2003, at 10.5 per thousand, was almost twice that for upstate New York, 5.7 per thousand. (Excluding delinquent children from the total care in the state reduces the foster care rate per thousand to 7.2 in 2003 and the comparable 2000 figure to 6.7.)

Dependent and neglected children made up about 95 percent of the total number in foster family homes and voluntary institutions in the state at the end of 2003, as they did in 2000. Delinquent children sent into care (outside the state training school system) by the Family Court accounted for only 5 percent of the total. The number of delinquent children in care rose 5 percent, as an increase in the state, 28 percent, more than offset a 13 percent decline in the city. Delinquents comprised 4.9 percent of the total number of children in care upstate at the end of 2003 and 3.9 percent in the city.

14. I. There were 45,000 children in care away from their own homes over the 2000-2003 period.
    II. The percentage decline of delinquent children in care in the city in 2003 was offset by a greater increase in the rest of the state.

    14.____

15. I. The increase in delinquent care in the state from 2000 to 2003 cannot be determined from the data given.
    II. The state's foster care rate in 2003, exclusive of the city, was about one-half the rate for the city

    15.____

16. I. In 2000 and in 2003, the percentage of dependent and neglected children in foster family homes and voluntary institutions in the state was about the same
    II. In 2000, the number of dependent and neglected children in foster family homes and voluntary institutions in the state was 43,250

    16.____

17. I. The city's child population rose approximately three percent from 2000 to 2003.
    II. At the end of 2003, less than 1% of the children 18 years of age or younger were in care.

    17.____

18. I. Delinquents in the city comprised 4.4 percent of the total number of children in care in the city at the end of 2000.
    II. An unsubstantial number of children living outside their own homes were placed by their parents or relatives without the assistance of a social agency.

    18.____

Questions 19-25.

DIRECTIONS: Questions 19 through 25 are to be answered SOLELY on the basis of the information contained in the following paragraph. Each question consists of a statement. You are to indicate whether the statement is TRUE (T) or FALSE (F).

RESPONSIBILITY OF PARENTS

In a recent survey, ninety percent of the people interviewed felt that parents should be held responsible for the delinquency of their children. Forty-eight out of fifty states have laws holding parents criminally responsible for contributing to the delinquency of their children. It is generally accepted that parents are a major influence in the early moral development of their children. Yet, in spite of all this evidence, practical experience seems to prove that *punish the parents* laws are wrong. Legally, there is some question about the constitutionality of such laws. How far can one person be held responsible for the actions of another? Further, although there are many such laws, the fact remains that they are rarely used and where they are used, they fail in most cases to accomplish the end for which they were intended.

19. Nine out of ten of those interviewed held that parents should be responsible for the delinquency of their children.

    19.____

20. Forty-eight percent of the states have laws holding parents responsible for contributing to the delinquency of their children.   20._____

21. Most people feel that parents have little influence on the early moral development of their children.   21._____

22. Experience seems to indicate that laws holding parents responsible for children's delinquency are wrong.   22._____

23. There is no doubt that laws holding parents responsible for delinquency of their children are within the Constitution.   23._____

24. Laws holding parents responsible for delinquent children are not often enforced.   24._____

25. *Punish the parent* laws usually achieve their purpose.   25._____

KEY (CORRECT ANSWERS)

1. A
2. D
3. D
4. C
5. B

6. B
7. C
8. A
9. A
10. B

11. C
12. D
13. C
14. B
15. B

16. A
17. D
18. D
19. T
20. F

21. F
22. T
23. F
24. T
25. F

TEST 2

DIRECTIONS: Each question or incomplete statement is followed by several suggested answers or completions. Select the one that BEST answers the question or completes the statement. *PRINT THE LETTER OF THE CORRECT ANSWER IN THE SPACE AT THE RIGHT.*

Questions 1-3.

DIRECTIONS: Questions 1 through 3 are to be answered SOLELY on the basis of the following passage.

    Undoubtedly, the ultimate solution to the housing problem of the hard-core slum does not lie in code enforcement, however defined. The only solution to that problem is demolition, clearance, and new construction. However, it is also clear that, even with government assistance, new construction is not keeping pace with the obsolescence and deterioration of the existing housing inventory of our cities. Add to this the facts of an increasing population and the continuing migration into metropolitan areas, as well as the demands for more and better housing that grow out of continuing economic prosperity and high employment, and some intimation may be gained of the dimensions of the problem of maintaining our housing supply so that it may begin to meet the need.

1. The one of the following that would be the MOST appropriate title for the above passage is
    A. PROBLEMS ASSOCIATED WITH MAINTAINING AN ADEQUATE HOUSING SUPPLY
    B. DEMOLITION AS A REMEDY FOR HOUSING PROBLEMS
    C. GOVERNMENT'S ESSENTIAL ROLE IN CODE ENFORCEMENT
    D. THE ULTIMATE SOLUTION TO THE HARD-CORE SLUM PROBLEM

1.____

2. According to the above passage, housing code enforcement is
    A. a way to encourage local initiative in urban renewal
    B. a valuable tool that has fallen into disuse
    C. inadequate as a solution to slum housing problems
    D. responsible for some of the housing problems since the code has not been adequately defined

2.____

3. The above passage makes it clear that the BASIC solution to the housing problem is to
    A. erect new buildings after demolition and site clearance
    B. discourage migration into the metropolitan area
    C. increase rents paid to landlords
    D. enforce the housing code strictly

3.____

Questions 4-5.

DIRECTIONS: Questions 4 and 5 are to be answered on the basis of the following passage.

Under common law, the tenant was obliged to continue to pay rent, at the risk of eviction, regardless of the condition of the premises. This obligation was based on the following established common law principles: first, that in the absence of express agreement, a lease does not contain any implied warrant of fitness or habitability; second, that the person in possession of premises has the obligation to repair and maintain them; and third, that a lease conveys an interest in real estate rather than binding one to a mutual obligation. Once having conveyed his property, the landlord's right to rent was unconditional. Thus, even if he made an express agreement to repair, the landlord's right to rent remained independent of his promise to repair. This doctrine, known as the *independence of covenant*, required the tenant to continue to pay rent or risk eviction, and to bring a separate action against the landlord for damages resulting from his breach of agreement to repair.

4. According to the above passage, common law provided that a lease would
    A. bar an ex parte action
    B. bind the parties thereto to a reciprocal obligation
    C. provide an absolute defense for breach of agreement
    D. transmit an interest in real property

5. According to the above passage, the *independence of covenants* required that the
    A. tenant continue to pay rent even for unfit housing
    B. landlord hold rents in escrow for aggrieved tenants
    C. landlord show valid cause for non-performance of lease requirements
    D. tenant surrender the demised premises in improved condition

Questions 6-11.

DIRECTIONS: Questions 6 through 11 are to be answered SOLELY on the basis of the information given in the following passage.

The City of X has set up a Maximum Base Rent Program for all rent-controlled apartments. The objective is to insure that the landlord will get a fair, but not excessive, profit on his building to stem the great tide of buildings being abandoned by their owners, and to encourage landlords to continue the upkeep of their property. The Maximum Base Rent Program permits the landlord to raise rents under carefully devised standards, while practically no raises in rents in this City were permitted under previous guidelines.

Under this plan, the City determines a Maximum Base Rent amount by means of a formula which takes into account the age of the building, the number of apartments, total rents received from the building, the amount of expenses, and labor costs. The Maximum Base Rent amount is to be recomputed every two year to allow for increases or decreases in building costs.

The Maximum Base Rent, which will allow the landlord to make a *fair return* on his investment, may not be collected immediately, however, since no rent increases over 7.5 percent will be permitted in any one year. The highest actual rent for each apartment during a given year will be called the Maximum Collectible Rent. This will be computed so that the increase over the present rent is not more than 7.5 percent ($7.50 on every $100.00). Sometimes, it may be less. Therefore, collectible rents will increase each year until the Maximum Base Rent is reached.

6. According to the above passage, the Maximum Base Rent is determined by the   6.____
   A. landlord
   B. Mayor
   C. Rent Commissioner
   D. City

7. Which of the following, according to the above passage, permits a *fair return* on the landlord's investment?   7.____
   The _____ Rent Program.
   A. Minimum Base
   B. Maximum Bass
   C. Minimum Collectible
   D. Maximum Collectible

8. It may be concluded from the above passage that the City of X hopes that insuring fair profits for landlords will be followed by   8.____
   A. good upkeep of apartment buildings
   B. decreased interest rates on home mortgages
   C. lower rents in the future
   D. a better formula for determining rents

9. According to the above passage, guidelines for determining rents previous to the Maximum Base Rent Program resulted in   9.____
   A. practically no raises in rents being made
   B. rent increases of approximately 10 percent a year
   C. a *fair return* to landlords from most rents
   D. landlords making too much money on their property

10. Based on the above passage, which is the MOST correct description of the kinds of facts that are taken into consideration when determining the Maximum Base Rent?   10.____
    Facts about
    A. labor costs and politics
    B. the landlord and labor costs
    C. the building and labor costs
    D. the building and the landlord

11. According to the above passage, the MAXIMUM annual increase in rent for a tenant in rent-controlled housing under the Maximum Base Rent Program is   11.____
    A. 7.5 percent each year for ten years
    B. 7.5 percent each year until the Maximum Base Rent is reached
    C. always under 7.5 percent a year
    D. $7.50 each year until it reaches $100.00

Questions 12-15.

DIRECTIONS: Questions 12 through 15 are to be answered SOLELY on the basis of the information contained in the following paragraph.

In all projects (except sites), when the Manager determines that a vacant apartment is to be permanently removed from the rent roll for any reason, e.g., the apartment has been converted to an office or community space, he shall notify the cashier by memorandum. The cashier shall enter the reduction in dwelling units in the Rent Control Book as of the first of the month following the date on which the apartment was vacated. He shall also prepare a reduction in Rent Roll (Form 105.046), the original of which is to be attached to the file copy of the Project Monthly Summary for the month during which the reduction is effective. Copies are to be sent to the Finance and Audit Department, Budget Section, and to the Chief of Insurance.

12. The purpose of the above paragraph is to provide for a procedure in handling   12.____
    A. the accounting for space occupied by offices and community centers
    B. apartments not rented as of the first of the month following the date on which the apartment was vacated
    C. vacant apartment temporarily used as office space
    D. vacant apartment permanently removed from the rent roll

13. The Rent Control Book is a control on the amount of monthly rents charged.   13.____
    According to the above paragraph, another function of the Rent Control Book is to indicate the
    A. number of offices and community spaces available in the project
    B. number of dwelling units in the project
    C. number of vacant apartments in the project
    D. rental loss for all offices and community spaces

14. In accordance with the above paragraph, the original of the Form 105.046 is   14.____
    to be
    A. sent to Central Office with the Project Monthly Summary
    B. kept in the project files with the project copy of the Project Monthly Summary
    C. sent to the Finance and Audit Department
    D. sent to the Chief of Insurance

15. The MOST likely reason for informing the Chief of Insurance of the removal of   15.____
    an apartment from the rent roll is to notify him
    A. to make adjustments in the insurance coverage
    B. of a future change in the address of the office or community space
    C. of a change in the project rent income
    D. of a possible increase in the number of project employees

Questions 16-20.

DIRECTIONS: Questions 16 through 20 are to be answered SOLELY on the basis of the information provided in the following passage.

It is the Housing Administration's policy that all tenants, whether new or transferring from one housing development to another, should be required to pay a standard security deposit of one month's rent based on the rent at the time of admission. There are, however, certain exceptions to this policy. Employees of the Administration shall not be required to pay a security deposit if they secure an apartment in an Administration development. Where the payment of a full security deposit may present a hardship to a tenant, the development's manager may allow a tenant to move into an apartment upon payment of only part of the security deposit. In such cases, however, the tenant must agree to gradually pay the balance of the deposit. If a tenant transfers from one apartment to another within the same project, the security deposit originally paid by the tenant for his former apartment will be acceptable for his new apartment, even if the rent in the new apartment is greater than the rent in the former one. Finally, tenants who receive public assistance need not pay a security deposit before moving into an apartment if the appropriate agency states, in writing, that it will pay the deposit. However, it is the responsibility of the development's manager to make certain that payment shall be received within one month of the date that the tenant moves into the apartment.

16. According to the above passage, when a tenant transfers from one apartment to another in the same development, the Housing Administration will
    A. accept the tenant's old security deposit as the security deposit for his new apartment regardless of the new apartment's rent
    B. refund the tenant's old security deposit and not require him to pay a new deposit
    C. keep the tenant's old security deposit and require him to pay a new deposit
    D. require the tenant to pay a new security deposit based on the difference between his old rent and his new rent

17. On the basis of the above passage, it is INCORRECT to state that a tenant who receives public assistance may move into an Administration development if
    A. he pays the appropriate security deposit
    B. the appropriate agency gives a written indication that it will pay the security deposit before the tenant moves in
    C. the appropriate agency states, by telephone, that it will pay the security deposit
    D. the appropriate agency writes the manager to indicate that the security deposit will be paid within one month but not less than two weeks from the date the tenant moves into the apartment

18. On the basis of the above passage, a tenant who transfers from an apartment in one development to an apartment in a different development will
    A. forfeit his old security deposit and be required to pay another deposit
    B. have his old security deposit refunded and not have to pay a new deposit
    C. pay the difference between his old security deposit and the new one
    D. have to pay a security deposit based on the new apartment's rent

19. The Housing Administration will NOT require payment of a security deposit if a tenant
    A. is an Administration employee
    B. is receiving public assistance
    C. claims that payment will present a hardship
    D. indicates, in writing, that he will be responsible for any damage done to his apartment

20. Of the following, the BEST title for the above passage is: 20.____
    A. SECURITY DEPOSITS – TRANSFERS
    B. SECURITY DEPOSITS – POLICY
    C. EXEMPTIONS AND EXCEPTIONS – SECURITY DEPOSITS
    D. AMOUNTS – SECURITY DEPOSITS

Questions 21-23.

DIRECTIONS: Questions 21 through 23 are to be answered SOLELY on the basis of the following paragraphs.

In our program, we must continually strive to increase public good will and to maintain that good will which we have already established. It is important to remember in all your public contacts that to a good many people you are the Department. Don't take out any of your personal gripes on the public. When we must appeal to the public for cooperation, that is when any good will we have built up will come in handy. If the public has been given incorrect or incomplete help when seeking information or advice, or have received what they considered poor treatment in dealing with members of the Department, they will not provide a sympathetic audience when we direct our appeals to them.

One of the Department activities in which there is considerable contact with the public is inspection. Any activity in this area poses special problems and makes your personal dealings with the individuals involved very important. You must bear in mind that you are dealing with people who are sensitive to the manner in which they are treated and you should guide yourself accordingly.

Let us consider some of the aspects of the actual inspection of the premises:

APPEARANCE: Your appearance will determine the initial impression made on anyone you deal with. It is often difficult to change a person's first impression, so try to make it a favorable one. Be neat and clean, show that you have taken some trouble to make a good appearance. Your appearance should form a part of a business-like attitude that should govern your inspection of any premises.

APPROACH: Be courteous at all times. When you enter a building, immediately seek out the owner or occupant and ask his permission to inspect the premises. Ask him to accompany you on the inspection if he has the time, and explain to him the reasons why such inspections are made. Try to give him the feeling that this is a cooperative effort and that his part in this effort is appreciated. Do not make your approach on the basis that it is your legal right to inspect the premises; a coercive attitude tends to produce a hostile reaction.

21. Of the following, the BEST title for the subject covered in the above paragraphs is 21.____
    A. GOOD MANNERS   B. PUBLIC RELATIONS
    C. NEATNESS   D. INSPECTIONAL DUTIES

22. According to the above paragraph, the FIRST impression an inspector makes on the public is that of 22.____
    A. sympathy   B. courtesy
    C. cleanliness and dress D. business attitude

23. According to the above paragraphs, if you want the public to cooperate with you, 23.____
you must
    A. be available at all times
    B. be sure that any information you give them is correct
    C. make sure that their complaints are justified
    D. be stern in your dealings with landlords

Questions 24-25.

DIRECTIONS: Questions 24 and 25 are to be answered SOLELY on the basis of the following passage.

There is no simple solution for controlling crime and deviant behavior. There is no panacea for anti-social conduct. The sooner society gives up the search for a single control solution, the sooner society will be able to face up to the immensity of the task and the never-ending responsibility of our social structure.

24. Which of the following statements is BEST supported by the above passage? 24.____
    A. Although crime causation may be considered singular, crime control is many-faceted.
    B. When society faces up to the immensity of the crime problem, it will find a single solution to it.
    C. A multi-faceted approach to crime control is better than trying to find a single cause or cure.
    D. Our social structure is responsible for a continuing search for a simple solution to anti-social behavior.

25. The crime problem can be solved when 25.____
    A. it is realized that no solution exists
    B. the problem is specifically identified
    C. criminals are punished
    D. none of the above

KEY (CORRECT ANSWERS)

1. A
2. C
3. A
4. D
5. A

6. D
7. B
8. A
9. A
10. C

11. B
12. D
13. B
14. B
15. A

16. A
17. C
18. D
19. A
20. B

21. B
22. C
23. B
24. C
25. D

ARITHMETICAL REASONING
EXAMINATION SECTION
TEST 1

DIRECTIONS: Each question or incomplete statement is followed by several suggested answers or completions. Select the one that BEST answers the question or completes the statement. *PRINT THE LETTER OF THE CORRECT ANSWER IN THE SPACE AT THE RIGHT.*

1. On January 1, a family was receiving supplementary monthly public assistance of $280 for food, $240 for rent, and $140 for other necessities. In the spring, their rent rose by 10%, and their rent allotment was adjusted accordingly. In the summer, due to the death of a family member, their allotments for food and other necessities were reduced by 1/7.
   Their monthly allowance check in the fall should be
   A. $623   B. $644   C. $664   D. $684   1.____

2. Twice a month, a certain family receives a $340 general allowance for rent, food, and clothing expense. In addition, the family receives a specific supplementary allotment for utilities of $384 a year, which is added to their semi-monthly check.
   If the general allowance alone is reduced by 5%, what will be the TOTAL amount of their next semi-monthly check?
   A. $323   B. $339   C. $340   D. $355   2.____

3. If each supervising clerk in a certain unit sees an average of 9 clients in a 7-hour day and there are 15 supervising clerks in the unit, APPROXIMATELY how many clients will be seen in a 35-hour week?
   A. 315   B. 405   C. 675   D. 945   3.____

4. In one day, an aide receives 18 inquiries by phone and 27 inquiries in person. What percentage of the inquiries received that day were by phone?
   A. 33%   B. 40%   C. 45%   D. 60%   4.____

5. If the weekly paychecks for 5 employees are $258.64, $325.48, $287.50, and $313.12, then the combined weekly income for the 5 employee is
   A. $1,455.68   B. $1,456.08   C. $1,462.68   D. $1,474.08   5.____

6. Suppose that there are 17 aides working in an office where many community complaints are received by telephone. In one ten-day period, 4,250 calls were received.
   If the same number of calls were received each day and the aides divided the work load equally, about how many calls did each aide respond to daily?
   A. 25   B. 35   C. 75   D. 250   6.____

7. Suppose that an assignment was divided among 5 aides.
   If the first aide spent 67 hours on the assignment, the second aide spent 95 hours, the third aide spent 52 hours, the fourth aide spent 78 hours, and the fifth aide spent 103 hours, what was the AVERAGE amount of time spent by each aide on the assignment? _____ hours.
   A. 71   B. 75   C. 79   D. 83

8. If there are 240 employees in a center and 1/3 are absent on the day of a bad snowstorm, how many employees were at work in the center on that day?
   A. 80   B. 120   C. 160   D. 200

9. Suppose that an aide takes 25 minutes to prepare a letter to a client.
   If the aide is assigned to prepare 9 letters on a certain day, how much time should be set aside for this task? _____ hours.
   A. 3¾   B. 4¼   C. 4¾   D. 5¼

10. Suppose that a certain center uses both Form A and Form B in the course of its daily work and that Form A is used 4 times as often as Form B.
    If the total number of both forms used in one week is 750, how many times was Form A used?
    A. 100   B. 200   C. 400   D. 600

11. Suppose a center has a budget of $2,185.40 from which 8 desks costing $156.10 apiece must be bought.
    How many additional desks can be ordered from this budget after the 8 desks have been purchased?
    A. 4   B. 6   C. 9   D. 14

12. When researching a particular case, a team of 16 aides was asked to check through 234 folders to obtain the necessary information.
    If half the aides worked twice as fast as the other half, and the slow group checked through 12 folders each hour, about how long would it take to complete the assignment? _____ hours.
    A. 4¼   B. 5   C. 6   D. 6½

13. The difference in the cost of two typewriters is $56.64.
    If the less expensive typewriter costs $307.22, what is the cost of the other typewriter?
    A. $343.86   B. $344.06   C. $363.86   D. $364.06

14. At the start of a year, a family was receiving a public assistance grant of $382 twice a month, on the first and fifteenth of each month. On March 1, their rent allowance was decreased from $150 to $142 a month since they had moved to a smaller apartment. On August 1 their semi-monthly food allowance, which had been $80.40, was raised by 10%.
    In that year, the TOTAL amount of money disbursed to this family was
    A. $4,544.20   B. $6,581.40   C. $9,088.40   D. $9,168.40

3 (#1)

15. It is discovered that a client has received double public assistance for 2 months by having been enrolled at two service centers of the Department of Social Services. The client should have received $168 twice a month instead of the double amount. He now agrees to repay the money by equal deductions from his public assistance check over a period of 12 months.
What will the amount of his NEXT check be?
   A. $112   B. $140   C. $154   D. $160

16. Suppose a study is being made of the composition of 3,550 families receiving public assistance. Of the first 1,050 families reviewed, 18% had four or more children.
If, in the remaining number of families, the percentage with four or more children is half as high as the percentage in the group already reviewed, then the percentage of families with four or more children in the entire group of families is MOST NEARLY
   A. 12   B. 14   C. 16   D. 17

17. Suppose that food prices have risen 13%, and an increase of the same amount has been granted in the food allotment given to people receiving public assistance.
If a family has been receiving $810 a month, 35% of which is allotted for food, then the TOTAL amount of public assistance this family receives per month will be changed to
   A. $805.42   B. $840.06   C. $846.86   D. $899.42

18. Assume that the food allowance is to be raised 5% in August but will be retroactive for four months to April.
The retroactive allowance is to be divided into equal sections and added to the public assistance checks for August, September, October, November, and December.
A family which has been receiving $840 monthly, 40% of which was allotted for food, will receive what size check in August?
   A. $853.44   B. $856.80   C. $861.00   D. $870.24

19. A blind client, who receives $210 public assistance twice a month, inherits 14 shares of stock worth $180 each. The client is required to sell the stock and spend his inheritance before receiving more public assistance.
Using his public assistance allowance as a guide, how many months are his new assets expected to last?
   A. 6   B. 7   C. 8   D. 12

20. The Department of Social Services has 16 service centers. These centers may be divided into those which are downtown and those which are uptown. Two of the centers are special service centers and are downtown, while the remainder of the centers are general service centers. There is a total of 7 service centers downtown.
The percentage of the general service centers which are uptown is MOST NEARLY
   A. 56   B. 64   C. 69   D. 79

21. For six months, a family lived in a 4-room apartment where they paid $380 a month. They made an intrasite move to a 4-room apartment where they paid $85 per room a month for six months.
Comparing the two six-month periods, the TOTAL amount of money the family saved by making the intrasite was
    A. $240   B. $290   C. $430   D. $590

22. To calculate a tenant's usable income, you should make Social Security deductions of 4.4 percent on salary up to a maximum of $9,000 and State Disability deductions of .5 percent on salary up to $3,000.
What does a tenant's combined deduction amount to if his annual salary is $13,400?
    A. $411.00   B. $568.60   C. $619.60   D. $700.00

23. If the temporary relocation expenses for housing are set at $18 per day for one adult and $10 per day for each additional person in a room, how much money is allowed for a woman and four children temporarily relocated in one room for a period of six days?
    A. $168   B. $348   C. $378   D. $518

24. According to relocation policy, a family relocating to private housing from federally-aided or certain other sites will be granted a relocation payment. This payment equals the difference between 1/5 of the family's yearly income and the scheduled yearly rent for a standard apartment for their size family. Suppose a 2-person family whose yearly income is $12,900 has been unable to obtain public housing and so finds a one-bedroom private apartment. The scheduled rent for a one-bedroom apartment appropriate for their occupancy is $240 a month.
What payment will they receive?
    A. $240   B. $288   C. $300   D. $410

25. A family on a housing relocation site is paying $410 per month for rent. This represents 25% of their gross monthly income.
If the husband earns 4/5 of their total combined monthly income, how much does the wife earn per month?
    A. $328   B. $540   C. $1,280   D. $1,500

KEY (CORRECT ANSWERS)

1. A
2. B
3. C
4. B
5. B

6. A
7. C
8. C
9. A
10. D

11. B
12. D
13. C
14. D
15. B

16. A
17. C
18. D
19. A
20. B

21. A
22. A
23. B
24. C
25. A

SOLUTIONS TO PROBLEMS

1. After spring, the rent allotment should be $(240+24) = $264. After the summer, the reduced allotment for food and other necessities should be $[(280+140) − 1/7(280+140)] = $(420−1/7(420)) = $(420−60) = $360. The monthly check in the fall including rent, food, and other necessities should be $360 + $264 = $624.

2. Amount of general allowance in the family's semi-monthly check = $340. Amount of utilities allotment in the family's semi-monthly check: ($\frac{384}{12}$ × ½) = $16. Amount of general allowance in family' semi-monthly check after a 5% reduction = $340 less 5% of $340 = $(340−17) = $3223. Total amount of the next month's semi-monthly check: Reduced general allowance + utilities allotment = $323 + $16 = $339.

3. During 7 hours, a total of (15)(9) = 135 clients can be seen. Thus, in 35 hours, a total of (135)(5) = 675 clients will be seen.

4. 18(18+27) = .40 = 40%

5. $258.64 + $325.48 + $287.34 + $271.50 + $313.12 = $1,456.08

6. 4250/10 = 425 calls per day. Then, 425/17 = 25

7. (67+95+52+78+103)/5 = 79 hours

8. Number present = (240)(2/3) = 160

9. (25)(9) = 225 min. = 3 hrs. 45 min. = 3 ¾ hours

10. Let x, 1/4x = number of forms A, B, respectively. Then, x + 1/4x = 750. Solving, x = 600

11. $2,185.40 − (8)($156.10) = $936.60. Then, $936.60 ÷ $156.10 = 6 desks

12. Since the slow group did 12 folders each hour, the faster group did 24 folders each hour. Then, 234/(12+24) = 6 ½ hrs.

13. Expensive typewriter costs $307.22 + $56.64 = $363.86

14. For months of January and February, the amount the family receives is $(382×2×2) = $1528
    For months of March through July, the family receives $(764−8) × 5 = $3780
    For months August through December, the family receives $(756+16.08) × 5 = $3860.40
    The total amount of money disbursed to this family is $1528 + $3780 + $3860.40 = $9,168.40

15. The overpayment for 2 months = ($168)(4) = $672. If this is paid back over 12 months, each month's amount is reduced by $672/12 = $56. Then, each check (semi-monthly) is reduced by $28. His next check will be $168 − $28 = $140

7 (#1)

16. (1050)(.18) + (2500)(.09) = 414. Then, 414/3550 = 12%

17. ($810)(.35) = $283.50 originally allotted for food. The new food allotment = ($283.50)(1.13) = $320.355. The total assistance now = $810 − $283.50 + $320.355 = $846.855 or $846.86

18. ($840)(.40) = $336 per month for food. The new food allowance = ($336)(1.05) = $352.80 per month. The difference of $16.80 is retroactive to April, which means ($16.80)(9) = $151.20 additional money for August through December. Each check for these 5 months will be increased by $15.20/5 = 30.24. Thus, the check in August = $840 + 30.24 = $840 + 30.24 = $870.24

19. ($180)(14) = $2520. Then, $2520/$420 = 6 months

20. 5 general are downtown; 9 of 14 general are uptown; 9/14 ≈ 64%

21. ($85)(4) = $340 per month. Savings per month = $380 - $340 = $40 For six months, the savings = $240

22. ($9000(.044) + ($3000)(.005) = $411 total deductions

23. ($18+$40)(6) = $348 relocation expenses

24. ($240)(12) − (1/5)($12,900) = $300 relocation payment

25. $410 ÷ .25 = $1640. The wife earns (1640)(1/5) = $328 each month

TEST 2

DIRECTIONS: Each question or incomplete statement is followed by several suggested answers or completions. Select the one that BEST answers the question or completes the statement. *PRINT THE LETTER OF THE CORRECT ANSWER IN THE SPACE AT THE RIGHT.*

1. A project tenant who owns and drives a taxicab for living, reports for a three-month period an income of $6,250 after operating expenses of $1,300 have been considered. In addition, his tips are valued at 12% of his income before operating expenses.
   An estimate of his yearly income is MOST NEARLY
   A. $22,000   B. $23,000   C. $28,000
   D. $28,500   E. $29,000

2. The maximum annual subsidy which can be paid by the State toward the operation of any low-rent housing project is the sum of the annual interest on the total original loan or building the project and 1% of the portion of the loan actually spent.
   If the original loan for a project was $8,000,000 at 1¾% interest, but only $7,500,000 was actually spent, then the MAXIMUM annual subsidy is
   A. $140,000   B. $145,000   C. $215,000
   D. $220,000   E. $271,250

3. In 2020, the cost of repairs and maintenance at a certain housing project was $5,589 more than in 2019, representing an increase of 4.6%. A further increase at the same rate was anticipated for 2021.
   The cost of repairs and maintenance in 2021 was MOST NEARLY
   A. $127,100
   B. $132,700
   C. $132,900
   D. $133,000
   E. an amount which cannot be determined from the given data

4. Each day a delivery truck used by the Housing Authority travels 25 miles from a project to a storehouse and 25 miles on the return trip. It travels at the rate of 30 miles per hour going to the storehouse and at the rate of 20 miles per hour returning.
   The average rate, in miles per hour, for the roundtrip is MOST NEARLY
   A. 24
   B. 25
   C. 26
   D. the square root of 600
   E. an amount which cannot be determined from the given data

5. A report on the first 6,000 applications for apartments in a certain project containing 1,400 apartments indicated that those who were ineligible fell into four categories: 2,800 ineligible for reason A, 600 ineligible for reason B, 1,200 ineligible for reason C, and 400 ineligible for reason D.

2 (#2)

If the same proportions continue for the remaining 21,500 applications, then the percentage of eligible applicants who can be given apartments in the project is MOST NEARLY
A. 25   B. 30   C. 33   D. 40   E. 60

6. The number of applications for apartments in low-rent housing projects was 40,000 in 2019. The number of applications increased 5% in 2020, and increased again in 2021 by 6% over the 2,000 total.
The percentage by which the 2021 figures exceed the 2019 figures is
A. 5.3   B. 6.0   C. 11.0   D. 11.3   E. 30.0

7. A rectangular lot, 75 feet by 11.0 feet, was purchased as part of a project site for $28,500.
The price per square foot of this lot is MOST NEARLY
A. $2.85   B. $3.45   C. $3.95   D. $30.00   E. $30.95

8. It has been estimated that 125 kilowatt-hours of electricity are used each month in one average Housing Authority apartment at a cost of 14.8 cents per kilowatt-hour.
On this basis, the total cost of the electricity used in one year in a project containing 1,400 apartments is MOST NEARLY
A. $20,000   B. $25,000   C. $200,000
D. $250,000   E. $2,000,000

9. The walls and ceilings of 20 rooms are to be painted with the same kind of paint, each room being 15 feet long, 12 feet wide, and 10 feet high. Each room contains two windows, each 3 feet by 6 feet, and a door 3 feet by 8 feet, which are not to be painted. One gallon of paint covers 400 square feet of surface.
The number of gallons of paint needed is MOST NEARLY
A. 33   B. 34   C. 35   D. 36   E. 75

10. A group of buildings is valued at $11,500,000. Assume that the cos of fire insurance for these buildings is 5.3 cents per $100 of valuation per year.
The cost of fire insurance for one year is MOST NEARLY
A. $600   B. $6,000   C. $20,000
D. $60,000   E. $2,000,000

11. Of the 15 employees in a certain unit, one-third earn $27,600 per year, three earn $32,600, one earns $46,400, and the rest earn $33,800.
The average salary of the employees of this unit is MOST NEARLY
A. $31,000   B. $32,000   C. $33,000   D. $34,000   E. $35,000

12. Four pieces, each 2'8½" long, are cut from a piece of pipe 16½' long.
The length of the remaining piece of pipe is
A. 6'8½"   B. 6'10"   C. 6'10³/₈"   D. 6'11¹/₈"   E. 9'9½"

3 (#2)

13. A tenant ears E dollars a month, spends S dollars a week, and saves the rest. The tenant's yearly savings can be expressed by
    A. 12(E-4S) B. 12E – 52S C. 12(E-S)
    D. 52(E-4S) E. E - S

14. A unit of fifteen Housing Assistants has been assigned the job of interviewing applicants. Each interview takes 35 minutes, and an additional 10 minutes is needed for making entries and notes. The last interview each day is always scheduled so that it can be completed that day.
    The number of applicants who can be interviewed in a week, consisting of five 7-hour days, is MOST NEARLY
    A. 375 B. 525 C. 675 D. 700 E. 725

15. A review of the 14,000 applications for apartments in a certain project containing 1,200 apartments indicated that 4,800 applicants were eligible and 6,400 were ineligible. No decision could be reached on the remaining applications because certain necessary information was omitted by the applicants, but it was assumed that the proportion of eligible and ineligible applicants would remain the same as in those already decided.
    On the basis of these figures, the percentage of eligible applicants who can be given apartments in the project is
    A. under 17% B. 17% C. 20%
    D. 25% E. 33 1/3%

16. An oil burner in a housing development burns 76 gallons of fuel oil per hour. At 9 A.M. on a very cold day, the superintendent asks the Housing Manager to put in an emergency order for more fuel oil. At that time, he reports that he has on hand 266 gallons. At noon, he again comes to the manager, notifying him that no oil has been delivered.
    The MAXIMUM amount of time that he can continue to furnish heat without receiving more oil is
    A. no more time B. ½ hour C. 1 hour
    D. 1½ hours E. 2 hours

17. As a result of reports received by the Housing Authority concerning the reputed ineligibility of 756 tenants because of above-standard incomes, an intensive check of their employers has been ordered. Four housing assistants have been assigned to this task. At the end of 6 days at 7 hours each, they have checked on 336 tenants. In order to speed up the investigation, two more housing assistants are assigned to this point.
    If they worked at the same rate, the number of additional 7-hour days it would take to complete the job is MOST NEARLY
    A. 1 B. 3 C. 5 D. 7 E. 9

4 (#2)

18. A municipal aide on a special trip is returning to his office from a point 17½ miles away, and makes the return trip to his office at an average speed of 25 miles an hour, except for a 15-minute stopover at one point to get a flat tire fixed. The time it should take him to reach his office is MOST NEARLY _____ minutes.
    A. 12   B. 22   C. 36   D. 42   E. 57

19. A district office has an assigned staff of 320 employees. Of this number, 25% are not available for duty due to illness, vacations, and other reasons. Of those who are available for duty, 1/8 are assigned to auditing and special projects, and the rest to handling the workload.
    The ACTUAL number of employees available for handling the workload is
    A. 350   B. 310   C. 270   D. 210   E. 180

20. Two dozen shuttlecocks and four badminton rackets are to be purchased for a playground. The shuttlecocks are priced at $3.60 each, and the rackets at $27.50 each. The playground receives a discount of 30% from these prices.
    The TOTAL cost of this equipment is
    A. $72.90   B. $114.30   C. $137.48   D. $186.00   E. $220.70

21. On January 1, a family was receiving public assistance allowance of $185 for food, $53 for clothing, $17.50 for utilities, and $22 for personal needs, all semi-monthly, and a monthly allowance of $550 for rent. On May 1, the rent allowance was increased by 12% but all other allowances remained the same for the rest of the year.
    The TOTAL amount of money granted this family during the year was
    A. $10,528   B. $13,262   C. $13,788
    D. $21,056   E. $27,676

22. It has been decided to make changes in food allotments to clients receiving public assistance to conform to changes in food costs. Of the food allowance, 30% is intended for meat, 30% for fruits and vegetables, 25% for groceries, and 15% for dairy products. Assume that meat prices have gone up 5%, and dairy prices have remained the same.
    For a family that has been receiving $400 per month for food, the new monthly food allowance will be
    A. $333   B. $375   C. $393   D. $403.50   E. $420

23. On January 1, a family was receiving a public assistance allowance of $195 for food, $63 for clothing, $27.50 for utilities, and $32 for personal needs, all semi-monthly, and a monthly allowance of $510 for rent. On June 1, the rent allowance was increased by 12%, but all other allowances remained the same for the rest of the year.
    The TOTAL amount of money granted this family during the year was
    A. $13,843.40   B. $14,107.20   C. $14,168.40
    D. $14,474.40   E. $16,886.80

24. A member of a family receiving public assistance amounting to $600 monthly has obtained a part-time job, for which he is paid $40 a day. He is employed 3 days a week. His carfare costs $3.00 per day and his lunches $2.00 per day. Assume that there are $4^1/_3$ weeks per month. The Department of Welfare requires that net earnings be deducted from relief allowances.
The family's semi-monthly public assistance allowances should be reduced to
 A. $40.00 B. $72.50 C. $96.25 D. $123.75 E. $145.00

24.____

25. A couple living in a furnished room has been receiving a public assistance grant of $375 semi-monthly and has been paying a weekly rent of $75. The landlord has been granted a 12% increase in rent. Assume that a month consists of $4^1/_3$ weeks.
The amount of the new semi-monthly grant, including this rent increase, that the couple will receive will be MOST NEARLY
 A. $394.50 B. $397 C. $409 D. $514 E. $557

25.____

KEY (CORRECT ANSWERS)

1.	D		11.	B
2.	C		12.	A
3.	C		13.	B
4.	A		14.	C
5.	B		15.	C
6.	D		16.	B
7.	B		17.	C
8.	D		18.	E
9.	A		19.	D
10.	B		20.	C

21.	C
22.	C
23.	C
24.	B
25.	A

SOLUTIONS TO PROBLEMS

1. For 3 months, income = $6,250 + (.12)($7550) = $7156. Then, annual income = ($7154)(4) = $28,624, closest to $28,500.

2. Maximum annual subsidy = ($8,000,000)(.0175) + (.01)($7,500,000) = $215,000

3. Cost in 2019 = $5589/.046 = $121,500. The cost in 2020 = $121,500 + $5589 = $127,089. This means the cost in 2021 = ($127,089)(1.046) = $132,900

4. Average rate = total distance/total time = (25+25) ÷ (25/30 + 25/20) = 24 mph

5. Out of 600, number of eligible = 6000 – 2800 – 600 – 1200 – 400 = 1000. Thus, for 27,500 applications, (1/6)(27,500) = 4583 would be eligible. Finally, 1400 ÷ 4583 ≈ 30%

6. Number of applications in 2020 = (40,000)(1.05) = 42,000. Number of applications in 2021 = (42,000)(1.06) = 44,520. Then, (44,520–40,000) ÷ 40,000 = 11.3%

7. $28,500 ÷ [(75×110)] = $3.45 per sq. ft.

8. Total cost = (125)(.148)(12)(1400) = $310,800; closest to choice D of $250,000

9. Painted area of each room = (2)(15)(10) + (2)(12)(10) + (15)(12) – (2)(3)(6) – (3)(8) = 660 sq. ft. So, (20)(660) = 13,200 sq. ft. to be painted in all rooms. Finally, 13,200/400 = 33 gallons of paint needed

10. Insurance cost = (.053)($11,500,000)/$100 = $6095, closest to $6000

11. [(5)($27,600) + (3)($32,600) + (1)($46,400) + (6)($33,800)]/15 = $32,233 closest to $32,000

12. 16½ - (4)(2'5³/₈") = 16'6" – 8'21½" = 16'6" – 9'9½" = 6'8½"

13. Annual savings = 12E – 52S

14. 7 ÷ ¾ = 9.$\overline{3}$, which means each interviewer can interview a maximum of 9 applicants each day. Then, (5)(9)(15) = 675 applicants

15. 4800/(4800+6400) = 3/7 eligible. On that assumption, there would be (3/7)(14,000) = 6000 eligible applicants. Then, 1200/6000 = 20%

16. 266 – (3)(76) = 38 gallons of oil left. Then, 38/76 = ½ hour

17. (6)(7)(4) = 168 hours to check on 336 tenants. This means 2 tenants require 1 man-hour. Now, (6)(7)(x days) = man-hours would be needed to check the remaining 420 tenants. This requires 210 man-hours. So, (6)(7)(x) = 210. Solving, x = 5

18. $\frac{17.5}{25}$ = .7 hr. = 42 min. Total time = 42 + 15 = 57 minutes.

7 (#2)

19. Number available = 320[1−.25(1/8)(.75) = 210

20. Total cost = (.70)[(24)($3.60)+(4)(27.50)] = $137.48

21. From January through April, amount = (8)($185+$53+$17.50+$22) + (4)($550) = $4420. From May through December, amount = (16)($185+$53+17.50+$22) + (8)($550)(1.12) = $9368. Total annual amount = $4420 + $9368 = $13,788

22. Meat allowance = ($400)(.30)(1.10) = $132; fruit and vegetable allowance = ($400)(.30)(.80) = $96; grocery allowance = ($400)(.25)(1.05) = $105; dairy allowance = ($400)(.15) = $60. New monthly allowance = $132 + $96 + $105 + $.60 = $393

23. From January through May, amount = (10)($195+$63+$27.50+$32) + (5)($510) = $5725. From June through December, amount = (14)($195+$63+$27.50+$32) + (7)($510)(1.12) = $8443.40. Total annual amount = $5725 + $8443.40 = $14,168.40

24. Monthly assistance should be reduced to $600 − [(40)(3)($4^{1}/_{3}$) − ($5)(3)($4^{1}/_{3}$)] = $145. So, the semi-monthly amount is now $145/2 = $72.50

25. ($75)($4^{1}/_{3}$)/2 = original semi-monthly rent.
New semi-monthly rent = (162.50)(1.12) = $182. Since this represents an increase of $19.50, the new semi-monthly grant will be increased to $375 + $19.50 = $394.50

PREPARING WRITTEN MATERIAL

PARAGRAPH REARRANGEMENT
COMMENTARY

The sentences that follow are in scrambled order. You are to rearrange them in proper order and indicate the letter choice containing the correct answer at the space at the right.

Each group of sentences in this section is actually a paragraph presented in scrambled order. Each sentence in the group has a place in that paragraph; no sentence is to be left out. You are to read each group of sentences and decide upon the best order in which to put the sentences so as to form a well-organized paragraph.

The questions in this section measure the ability to solve a problem when all the facts relevant to its solution are not given.

More specifically, certain positions of responsibility and authority require the employee to discover connection between events sometimes, apparently, unrelated. In order to do this, the employee will find it necessary to correctly infer that unspecified events have probably occurred or are likely to occur. This ability becomes especially important when action must be taken on incomplete information.

Accordingly, these questions require competitors to choose among several suggested alternatives, each of which presents a different sequential arrangement of the events. Competitors must choose the MOST logical of the suggested sequences.

In order to do so, they may be required to draw on general knowledge to infer missing concepts or events that are essential to sequencing the given events. Competitors should be careful to infer only what is essential to the sequence. The plausibility of the wrong alternatives will always require the inclusion of unlikely events or of additional chains of events which are NOT essential to sequencing the given events.

It's very important to remember that you are looking for the best of the four possible choices, and that the best choice of all may not even be one of the answers you're given to choose from.

There is no one right way to solve these problems. Many people have found it helpful to first write out the order of the sentences, as they would have arranged them, on their scrap paper before looking at the possible answers. If their optimum answer is there, this can save them some time. If it isn't, this method can still give insight into solving the problem. Others find it most helpful to just go through each of the possible choices, contrasting each as they go along. You should use whatever method feels comfortable and works for you.

While most of these types of questions are not that difficult, we've added a higher percentage of the difficult type, just to give you more practice. Usually there are only one or two questions on this section that contain such subtle distinctions that you're unable to answer confidently. And you then may find yourself stuck deciding between two possible choices, neither of which you're sure about.

EXAMINATION SECTION
TEST 1

DIRECTIONS: Each group of sentences in this section is actually a paragraph presented in scrambled order. Each sentence in the group has a place in that paragraph; no sentence is to be left out. You are to read each group of sentences so as to form a well-organized paragraph. Before trying to answer the questions which follow each group of sentences, jot down the correct order of the sentences. Then answer each of the questions by printing the letter of the correct answer in the space at the right. Remember that you will receive credit only for answers marked.

P. It is unfounded because, while the weak resent the power of the strong, they also respect it.
Q. The hesitancy stems from a concern for public opinion in other countries.
R. The United States has ordinarily been ill at ease in using its military power in support of its interests.
S. The concern is largely unfounded.
T. The roots of American hesitancy are deeply imbedded in the American mind.

1. Which sentence did you put last?
   A. P B. Q C. R D. S E. T

2. Which sentence did you put after Sentence R?
   A. P
   B. Q
   C. S
   D. T
   E. None of the above. Sentence R is last.

3. Which sentence did you put before Sentence S?
   A. P
   B. Q

4. Which sentence did you put before Sentence R?
   A. P
   B. Q
   C. S
   D. T
   E. None of the above. Sentence R is last.

5. Which sentence did you put fourth?
A. P   B. Q   C. R   D. S   E. T

KEY (CORRECT ANSWERS)

1. A
2. D
3. B
4. E
5. D

TEST 2

DIRECTIONS: Each group of sentences in this section is actually a paragraph presented in scrambled order. Each sentence in the group has a place in that paragraph; no sentence is to be left out. You are to read each group of sentences so as to form a well-organized paragraph. Before trying to answer the questions which follow each group of sentences, jot down the correct order of the sentences. Then answer each of the questions by printing the letter of the correct answer in the space at the right. Remember that you will receive credit only for answers marked.

P. Its lawlessness was virtually non-existent.
Q. The *Old West*, as portrayed in motion pictures, on television, and in books, is completely distorted.
R. It is obvious, therefore, that the *Old West* is falsely presented in mass media solely for commercial purposes.
S. Its heroes, too, were far from heroic.
T. Those who lived in the *Old West* in its final days, or talked to oldtimers, know the truth.

1. Which sentence did you put last?
   A. P   B. Q   C. R   D. S   E. T

2. Which sentence did you put after Sentence Q?
   A. P
   B. R
   C. S
   D. T
   E. None of the above. Sentence Q is last.

3. Which sentence did you put before Sentence S?
   A. P
   B. Q
   C. R
   D. T
   E. None of the above. Sentence S is first.

4. Which sentence did you put before Sentence Q?
   A. P
   B. R
   C. S
   D. T
   E. None of the above. Sentence Q is first.

5. Which sentence did you put after Sentence S? 5._____
   A. P
   B. Q
   C. R
   D. T
   E. None of the above. Sentence S is last.

KEY (CORRECT ANSWERS)

1. C
2. D
3. A
4. E
5. C

TEST 3

DIRECTIONS: Each group of sentences in this section is actually a paragraph presented in scrambled order. Each sentence in the group has a place in that paragraph; no sentence is to be left out. You are to read each group of sentences so as to form a well-organized paragraph. Before trying to answer the questions which follow each group of sentences, jot down the correct order of the sentences. Then answer each of the questions by printing the letter of the correct answer in the space at the right. Remember that you will receive credit only for answers marked.

P. One advertising executive became agitated recently when he suddenly realized that the floors of supermarkets were being unimaginatively used merely to walk on.
Q. Blank spaces, advertising men feel, cry out to be filled with merchandise-hustling messages.
R. He invented a slide projector which projects images on sheets of translucent plastic embedded in supermarket floors.
S. At once, he got to work to correct this unforgiveable oversight.
T. As nature abhors a vacuum, so do advertising men decry blank spaces.

1. Which sentence did you put last?
   A. P
   B. Q
   C. S
   D. T
   E. None of the above. Sentence R is last.

2. Which sentence did you put third?
   A. P   B. Q   C. R   D. S   E. T

3. Which sentence did you put before Sentence T?
   A. P
   B. Q
   C. R
   D. T
   E. None of the above. Sentence T is first.

4. Which sentence did you put after Sentence P?
   A. Q
   B. R
   C. S
   D. T
   E. None of the above. Sentence P is last.

5. Which sentence did you put before Sentence Q? 5.____
    A. P
    B. R
    C. S
    D. T
    E. None of the above. Sentence Q is last.

KEY (CORRECT ANSWERS)

1. E
2. A
3. E
4. C
5. D

TEST 4

DIRECTIONS: Each group of sentences in this section is actually a paragraph presented in scrambled order. Each sentence in the group has a place in that paragraph; no sentence is to be left out. You are to read each group of sentences so as to form a well-organized paragraph. Before trying to answer the questions which follow each group of sentences, jot down the correct order of the sentences. Then answer each of the questions by printing the letter of the correct answer in the space at the right. Remember that you will receive credit only for answers marked.

P. It is estimated that Americans smoked almost a trillion cigarettes in 2020, while they smoked only several hundred million cigars and pipefuls of tobacco.
Q. Originally, they were considered exclusively a *ladies'* smoke.
R. Only in this century did cigarettes become popular in the United States.
S. Far more Americans smoke cigarettes today than smoke cigars and pipes combined.
T. This was not always the case, however.

1. Which sentence did you put first?
   A. P   B. Q   C. R   D. S   E. T

2. Which sentence did you put after Sentence Q?
   A. P
   B. R
   C. S
   D. T
   E. None of the above. Sentence Q is last.

3. Which sentence did you put before Sentence T?
   A. P
   B. Q
   C. R
   D. S
   E. None of the above. Sentence T is last.

4. Which sentence did you put after Sentence R?
   A. P
   B. Q
   C. S
   D. T
   E. None of the above. Sentence R is last.

5. Which sentence did you put before Sentence R?   5.____
   A. P
   B. Q
   C. S
   D. T
   E. None of the above. Sentence R is first.

KEY (CORRECT ANSWERS)

1. D
2. E
3. A
4. B
5. D

TEST 5

DIRECTIONS: Each group of sentences in this section is actually a paragraph presented in scrambled order. Each sentence in the group has a place in that paragraph; no sentence is to be left out. You are to read each group of sentences so as to form a well-organized paragraph. Before trying to answer the questions which follow each group of sentences, jot down the correct order of the sentences. Then answer each of the questions by printing the letter of the correct answer in the space at the right. Remember that you will receive credit only for answers marked.

P. A *megagram*, or a million *grams*, is, therefore, equal to 2.205 pounds.
Q. A *gram* is equivalent to 1/28.35 ounces.
R. The fundamental unit of mass in the metric system is the *gram*.
S. A *kilogram*, or a thousand *grams*, is equal to 2.205 pounds.
T. *Gram* is derived from the late Greek, *gramma*, meaning a *small weight*.

1. Which sentence did you put after Sentence S?
   A. P
   B. Q
   C. R
   D. T
   E. None of the above. Sentence S is last.

2. Which sentence did you put before Sentence T?
   A. P
   B. Q
   C. R
   D. S
   E. None of the above. Sentence T is first.

3. Which sentence did you put after Sentence Q?
   A. P
   B. R
   C. S
   D. T
   E. None of the above. Sentence Q is last.

4. Which sentence did you put before Sentence R?
   A. P
   B. Q
   C. S
   D. T
   E. None of the above. Sentence R is first.

5. Which sentence did you put after Sentence T?   5.____
    A. P
    B. Q
    C. R
    D. S
    E. None of the above. Sentence T is last.

    _____

KEY (CORRECT ANSWERS)

1. A
2. C
3. C
4. E
5. B

_____

PREPARING WRITTEN MATERIAL
EXAMINATION SECTION
TEST 1

DIRECTIONS: Each of the sentences in this test may be classified under one of the following four categories:
- A. *Incorrect* because of faulty grammar or sentence structure
- B. *Incorrect* because of faulty punctuation
- C. *Incorrect* because of faulty capitalization
- D. *Correct*

Examine each sentence carefully to determine under which of the above four options it is best classified. Then, in the space at the right, print the capital letter preceding the option which is the BEST of the four suggested above.

(Each incorrect sentence contains but one type of error. Consider a sentence to be correct if it contains none of the types of errors mentioned, even though there may be other correct ways of expressing the same thought.)

1. This fact, together with those brought out at the previous meeting, prove that the schedule is satisfactory to the employees.   1.____

2. Like many employees in scientific fields, the work of bookkeepers and accountants requires accuracy and neatness.   2.____

3. "What can I do for you," the secretary asked as she motioned to the visitor to take a seat.   3.____

4. Our representative, Mr. Charles will call on you next week to determine whether or not your claim has merit.   4.____

5. We expect you to return in the spring; please do not disappoint us.   5.____

6. Any supervisor, who disregards the just complaints of his subordinates, is remiss in the performance of his duty.   6.____

7. Because she took less than an hour for lunch is no reason for permitting her to leave before five o'clock.   7.____

8. "Miss Smith," said the supervisor, "Please arrange a meeting of the staff for two o'clock on Monday."   8.____

9. A private company's vacation and sick leave allowance usually differs considerably from a public agency.   9.____

10. Therefore, in order to increase the efficiency of operations in the department, a report on the recommended changes in procedures was presented to the departmental committee in charge of the program.   10.____

11. We told him to assign the work to whoever was available. 11._____

12. Since John was the most efficient of any other employee in the bureau, he received the highest service rating. 12._____

13. Only those members of the national organization who resided in the middle West attended the conference in Chicago. 13._____

14. The question of whether the office manager has as yet attained, or indeed can ever hope to secure professional status is one which has been discussed for years. 14._____

15. No one knew who to blame for the error which, we later discovered, resulted in a considerable loss of time. 15._____

KEY (CORRECT ANSWERS)

1.	A	6.	B	11.	D
2.	A	7.	A	12.	A
3.	B	8.	C	13.	C
4.	B	9.	A	14.	B
5.	D	10.	D	15.	A

TEST 2

DIRECTIONS: Each of the sentences in this test may be classified under one of the following four categories:
  A. *Incorrect* because of faulty grammar or sentence structure
  B. *Incorrect* because of faulty punctuation
  C. *Incorrect* because of faulty capitalization
  D. *Correct*

1. The National alliance of Businessmen is trying to persuade private businesses to hire youth in the summertime.   1.____

2. The supervisor who is on vacation, is in charge of processing vouchers.   2.____

3. The activity of the committee at its conferences is always stimulating.   3.____

4. After checking the addresses again, the letters went to the mailroom.   4.____

5. The director, as well as the employees, are interested in sharing the dividends.   5.____

KEY (CORRECT ANSWERS)

1. C
2. B
3. D
4. A
5. A

TEST 3

DIRECTIONS: In each of the following groups of sentences, one of the four sentences is faulty in grammar, punctuation, or capitalization. Select the INCORRECT sentence in each case.

1. A. Sailing down the bay was a thrilling experience for me.
   B. He was not consulted about your joining the club.
   C. This story is different than the one I told you yesterday.
   D. There is no doubt about his being the best player.

   1.____

2. A. He maintains there is but one road to world peace.
   B. It is common knowledge that a child sees much he is not supposed to see.
   C. Much of the bitterness might have been avoided if arbitration had been resorted to earlier in the meeting.
   D. The man decided it would be advisable to marry a girl somewhat younger than him.

   2.____

3. A. In this book, the incident I liked least is where the hero tries to put out the forest fire.
   B. Learning a foreign language will undoubtedly give a person a better understanding of his mother tongue.
   C. His actions made us wonder what he planned to do next.
   D. Because of the war, we were unable to travel during the summer vacation.

   3.____

4. A. The class had no sooner become interested in the lesson than the dismissal bell rang.
   B. There is little agreement about the kind of world to be planned at the peace conference.
   C. "Today," said the teacher, "we shall read 'The Wind in the Willows,' I am sure you'll like it.
   D. The terms of the legal settlement of the family quarrel handicapped both sides for many years.

   4.____

5. A. I was so surprised that I was not able to say a word.
   B. She is taller than any other member of the class.
   C. It would be much more preferable if you were never seen in his company.
   D. We had no choice but to excuse her for being late.

   5.____

144

KEY (CORRECT ANSWERS)

1. C
2. D
3. A
4. C
5. C

TEST 4

DIRECTIONS: In each of the following groups of sentences, one of the four sentences is faulty in grammar, punctuation, or capitalization. Select the INCORRECT sentence in each case.

1. A. Please send me these data at the earliest opportunity.
   B. The loss of their material proved to be a severe handicap.
   C. My principal objection to this plan is that it is impracticable.
   D. The doll had laid in the rain for an hour and was ruined.

   1.____

2. A. The garden scissors, left out all night in the rain, were in a badly rusted condition.
   B. The girls felt bad about the misunderstanding which had arisen
   C. Sitting near the campfire, the old man told John and I about many exciting adventures he had had.
   D. Neither of us is in a position to undertake a task of that magnitude.

   2.____

3. A. The general concluded that one of the three roads would lead to the besieged city.
   B. The children didn't, as a rule, do hardly anything beyond what they were told to do.
   C. The reason the girl gave for her negligence was that she had acted on the spur of the moment.
   D. The daffodils and tulips look beautiful in that blue vase.

   3.____

4. A. If I was ten years older, I should be interested in this work.
   B. Give the prize to whoever has drawn the best picture.
   C. When you have finished reading the book, take it back to the library.
   D. My drawing is as good as or better than yours.

   4.____

5. A. He asked me whether the substance was animal or vegetable.
   B. An apple which is unripe should not be eaten by a child.
   C. That was an insult to me who am your friend.
   D. Some spy must of reported the matter to the enemy.

   5.____

6. A. Limited time makes quoting the entire message impossible.
   B. Who did she say was going?
   C. The girls in your class have dressed more dolls this year than we.
   D. There was such a large amount of books on the floor that I couldn't find a place for my rocking chair.

   6.____

7. A. What with his sleeplessness and his ill health, he was unable to assume any responsibility for the success of the meeting.
   B. If I had been born in February, I should be celebrating my birthday soon.
   C. In order to prevent breakage, she placed a sheet of paper between each of the plates when she packed them.
   D. After the spring shower, the violets smelled very sweet.

   7.____

8. A. He had laid the book down very reluctantly before the end of the lesson.
    B. The dog, I am sorry to say, had lain on the bed all night.
    C. The cloth was first lain on a flat surface; then it was pressed with a hot iron.
    D. While we were in Florida, we lay in the sun until we were noticeably tanned.

    8.____

9. A. If John was in New York during the recent holiday season, I have no doubt he spent most of the time with his parents.
    B. How could he enjoy the television program; the dog was barking and the baby was crying.
    C. When the problem was explained to the class, he must have been asleep.
    D. She wished that her new dress were finished so that she could go to the party.

    9.____

10. A. The engine not only furnishes power but light and heat as well.
    B. You're aware that we've forgotten whose guilt was established, aren't you?
    C. Everybody knows that the woman made many sacrifices for her children.
    D. A man with his dog and gun is a familiar sight in this neighborhood.

    10.____

KEY (CORRECT ANSWERS)

1. D   6. D
2. C   7. B
3. B   8. C
4. A   9. B
5. D   10. A

TEST 5

DIRECTIONS: Each of Questions 1 through 5 consists of a sentence which may be classified appropriately under one of the following four categories:
    A. *Incorrect* because of faulty grammar
    B. *Incorrect* because of faulty punctuation
    C. *Incorrect* because of faulty spelling
    D. *Correct*

Examine each sentence carefully. Then, print in the space at the right the letter preceding the category which is the BEST of the four suggested above
(Note: Each incorrect sentence contains only one type of error. Consider a sentence correct if it contains no errors, although there may be other correct ways of writing the sentence.)

1. Of the two employees, the one in our office is the most efficient.   1.____

2. No one can apply or even understand, the new rules and regulations.   2.____

3. A large amount of supplies were stored in the empty office.   3.____

4. If an employee is occassionally asked to work overtime, he should do so willingly.   4.____

5. It is true that the new procedures are difficult to use but, we are certain that you will learn them quickly.   5.____

6. The office manager said that he did not know who would be given a large allotment under the new plan.   6.____

7. It was at the supervisor's request that the clerk agreed to postpone his vacation.   7.____

8. We do not believe that it is necessary for both he and the clerk to attend the conference.   8.____

9. All employees, who display perseverance, will be given adequate recognition.   9.____

10. He regrets that some of us employees are dissatisfied with our new assignments.   10.____

11. "Do you think that the raise was merited," asked the supervisor?   11.____

12. The new manual of procedure is a valuable supplement to our rules and regulations.   12.____

13. The typist admitted that she had attempted to pursuade the other employees to assist her in her work.   13.____

14. The supervisor asked that all amendments to the regulations be handled by you and I.   14.____

15. The custodian seen the boy who broke the window.   15.____

KEY (CORRECT ANSWERS)

1.	A	6.	D	11.	B
2.	B	7.	D	12.	C
3.	A	8.	A	13.	C
4.	C	9.	B	14.	A
5.	B	10.	D	15.	A

www.ingramcontent.com/pod-product-compliance
Lightning Source LLC
Chambersburg PA
CBHW080324020526

44117CB00035B/2646